The CLASSICS

The CLASSICS

June Holm

Contents

Introduction

Every cook should have a cookbook that contains all the classic recipes that they love to eat and make for their family. In this brand new collection of everyday recipes you'll find soups, stews, pasta dishes, rice dishes, roasts, risottos, side dishes and a fabulous array of cakes, puddings, cookies and traybakes. Each and every recipe has stood the test of time as well as trends in contemporary cooking. There are recipes here that we remember from childhood – shepherd's pie, spaghetti Bolognese, quiche, fish pie - all presented here in one handy volume. So, whether you're cooking for one or for a party, are feeding a wide variety of age groups or faddy eaters, you're sure to find something within this collection that is suitable to serve.

The recipes are arranged according to meal, so there are recipes for an assortment of breakfasts, though I'm sure you'll agree that many of these recipes are perfect for a light snack or a simple lunch. Then there are soup recipes that include light and flavourful bisque to thick and filling cream of chicken, each suitable to serve up for a wide variety of occasions. The main courses that feature include pasta and rice dishes, a range of pies including pastry- and mash-topped varieties, and a whole host of roast dinners, all perfect to serve when you've got time to spare for preparation and cooking. Alongside these main courses is a chapter of everyday favourite side dishes. From French fries to jackets, minted peas and corn on the cob, there are nutritious and delicious recipes that fit perfectly with the main courses on offer. To finish your meal, or for a sweet and indulgent snack at any time there's a range of cakes, cookies, sophisticated desserts and hearty puddings to make and enjoy. So, sit back and let the beautiful photographs of each dish inspire your culinary creations and help you plan the weekly menu.

BREAKFAST

Breakfast

It's often said that breakfast is the most important meal of the day. And with good reason too. A small meal that contains some carbohydrate and protein is the best thing we can feed our body after a night's sleep. Food eaten first thing in the morning helps to kick start our metabolism, raises blood sugar levels and helps to keep us feeling warm and insulated. Without breakfast we might feel sluggish and hungry, and if we're hungry then it's difficult to concentrate on our work, our mood may take a downturn and our tolerance levels may start to fall. Food nourishes our bodies in so many ways, providing energy to sustain us, so eating the right foods at the most appropriate time, helps us to function efficiently.

Many of us eat the same breakfast day in day out. That might be because it's a food type that we like and having the same choice is easy, especially if we have busy routines and too many tasks to complete before we leave the house each day, or it might be a habit that we'd like to change. Weekday breakfasts might be rushed affairs, with all members of the household serving themselves and all eating at slightly different times. Weekend breakfasts, on the other hand, may be more leisurely affairs. They may be pitched at a slightly later time and be more lavish in their content to counter the more regulated schedule of the working week.

In this chapter you'll find many time-honoured recipes that embrace every type of traditional breakfast dish. Here, there is something for all tastes and all pockets: everyday dishes that you'll eat time and again, and seasonal treats that you'll reserve for those days when you've time and inclination to spare in preparing and cooking them.

Hot porridge is a grain dish that many of us remember from childhood. It's a staple, inexpensive dish that can be dressed up with any combination of sugar, cream, stewed fruits, fresh berries, dried fruits, seeds and ground nuts. For a skinny version make it with water and for an indulgent version add milk and serve with any combination listed above. For speed, you can cook it in the microwave. For traditionalists, it's made in a pan and cooked slowly over gentle heat.

For the super-organised among us, why not whip up a batch of pancake batter in the evening and leave it to rest overnight in the refrigerator? Spoon ladlesful into a hot pan, greased with a little oil and serve up light and fluffy pancakes as a treat one morning. These, too, can be dressed up or down with an assortment of poached, stewed and fresh fruits, syrups or chocolate spread. You could even add mashed or sliced banana into the pancake batter to ring the changes.

Bread, in many forms, is often a significant type of breakfast food. Toasted and spread with jam and butter, or presented as pikelets, crumpets, waffles or French toast, each has its own appeal. Take the time and try them homemade; they're almost always superior to shop-bought produce. And, while making your own from scratch takes time, you'll have the satisfaction of knowing exactly what ingredients have gone into its making, and that the item you make will be more filling and satisfying to eat, sustaining you for longer than the ready prepared item. Hot cross buns are one of life's pleasures; perhaps because they're seasonal and a tasty treat. Have fun making your own and you can tweak the spices and fruit to create a balance that your family will love.

Eggs have long been associated with breakfast. Served with toast they make a perfect combination that will keep you feeling full for longer. Eggs can be poached, scrambled, fried, boiled or made into an omelette. This versatile food has a universal appeal, and every imaginable recipe is presented here. Boil a couple of eggs and either present them with toast soldiers, or hard boil an egg and spread it on a slice of toast. If you like a decadent breakfast to linger over, then nothing beats eggs benedict. This poached egg with Hollandaise sauce combination can be served on toasted bread or muffins, with smoked salmon, ham or bacon – perfect for breakfast, brunch or lunch. It's rich and indulgent so great to serve on a special birthday or occasion.

Porridge

65 g (2¼ oz / ¾ cup) rolled oats
500 ml (17 fl oz / 2 cups) water
2 tablespoons brown sugar
75 ml (2 fl oz / ⅓ cup) milk

1. Place the oats and three-quarters of the water in a medium bowl. Cover and soak at room temperature overnight.
2. Transfer the oats and liquid to a medium saucepan. Add the remaining water and bring to the boil. Reduce the heat and simmer, stirring, for 10 minutes, or until the liquid has been absorbed. Divide the porridge between 2 serving bowls. Sprinkle with brown sugar and serve with cold milk.

serves 2

Cinnamon pancakes

115 g (4 oz / 1 cup) self-raising (self-rising) flour
50 g (1¾ oz / ¼ cup) caster (superfine) sugar
2 teaspoons cinnamon sugar
2 eggs, lightly beaten
175 ml (6 fl oz / ¾ cup) milk
oil cooking spray
strawberries and bananas, to serve
maple syrup
ice cream

1. Sift the flour into a mixing bowl. Add the sugar and cinnamon sugar. Make a well in the middle and add the eggs and milk. Slowly whisk the mixture until smooth.
2. Spray a non-stick frying pan with oil. Heat the frying pan over low to medium heat. Pour in a ladle of the mixture and cook the pancakes for 2 minutes on each side, or until cooked. Repeat with the remaining mixture.
3. Serve the pancakes topped with sliced strawberries and bananas. Drizzle with maple syrup and serve with scoops of ice cream.

makes 8

Pikelets

115 g (4 oz/1 cup) self-raising (self-rising) flour
pinch of salt
2 tablespoons sugar
1 egg
250 ml (8 fl oz/1 cup) milk
2 tablespoons butter
1 teaspoon golden (light corn) syrup
a little oil or butter, for greasing
butter, jam and cream, for serving

1. Sift the flour and salt into a bowl and add the sugar. Beat the egg and milk together and stir into the flour. Melt the butter and golden syrup together and stir over a low heat until melted, then add to the mixture.
2. Grease a griddle or shallow-frying pan with a little oil or butter and when it is hot, drop in the batter in spoonfuls (about a tablespoon), a little apart. Cook over a medium heat until the underside is browned and small bubbles appear on the surface, then turn and brown the other side. Serve warm with butter or cold with jam and whipped cream.

makes about 20

Crumpets

1. In a large bowl, add the flour, yeast, cream of tartar, salt and sugar and mix. Add the warm water and mix well until a thick batter forms. Knead well by hand until the dough is thick and smooth. Cover and allow to rise for 1 hour.
2. In a small bowl, add the bicarbonate of soda to the warm milk, mix well, and add to the dough, incorporating well so that there are no lumps.
3. Grease some crumpet rings and heat a frying pan over medium heat on the stovetop. Grease very lightly. Place the crumpet rings on the griddle and add 2 tablespoons of batter to each crumpet. (Test one crumpet first to check the consistency of the batter—holes should form in the surface of the dough after 3–4 minutes. If not, add a little more water to the batter, then proceed).
4. When the surface of dough is full of holes, remove the crumpet ring and, using a palette knife, turn the crumpet and fry the other side for a minute or two until light golden. Continue with the remaining batter. Serve with butter and honey, if you like.

serves 4

Waffles

60 g (2 oz / ½ cup) wholemeal (whole wheat) pastry flour
60 g (2 oz / ½ cup) plain (all-purpose) wholemeal (whole wheat) flour
2 egg whites
1½ tablespoons safflower oil
2 tablespoons apple sauce
2 tablespoons honey
¼ teaspoon salt
2 teaspoons baking powder
1 tablespoon soy milk

1. Mix all ingredients with a ladleful of water until just combined.
2. Heat a waffle iron. Pour in the batter until almost full, close and cook for approximately 4 minutes, or until golden brown.
3. Serve with fresh fruit of your choice and drizzled with maple syrup.

serves 4

French toast

1 egg
60 ml (2 fl oz / ¼ cup) milk
2 slices bread
butter, to serve

FOR SAVOURY TOAST
salt and freshly ground black pepper

FOR SWEET TOAST
1 tablespoon sugar
1 teaspoon vanilla extract
½ teaspoon ground cinnamon

1. Whisk together the egg and milk. For savoury toast, add season the milk mixture and whisk well. For sweet toast, add the sugar, vanilla extract and cinnamon to the milk mixture and whisk well.
2. Melt a knob of butter in a frying pan set over medium heat on the stovetop. Dip the bread slices in the egg mixture, covering both sides. Place in the pan and fry on both sides for a few minutes
3. Serve with your favourite breakfast spread.

serves 1

Hot cross buns

3 x 7 g (¼ oz) sachets dried yeast granules
250 ml (8 fl oz / 1 cup) lukewarm milk
pinch of salt
2 tablespoons light brown sugar
1 teaspoon ground cinnamon
½ teaspoon ground nutmeg
¼ teaspoon ground mixed (apple pie) spice
2 eggs
1 lb (450 g / 4 cups) plain (all-purpose) flour, plus extra for dusting

vegetable oil, for greasing
2 tablespoons mixed fruit peel
2 tablespoons raisins

FOR THE CROSS AND GLAZE
55 g (2 oz / ½ cup) plain (all-purpose) flour
½ teaspoon gelatine
2 tablespoons icing (confectioners') sugar
2 tablespoons no-fat (skimmed) milk, warmed

1. Place the yeast in a large bowl. Pour in the milk, mix together and set aside in warm place for 10 minutes, or until frothy. Stir in the salt, sugar and spices. Beat in the eggs, one at a time. Stir in half the flour to make a soft dough. Beat in oil. Continue beating for 1 minute. Knead in the remaining flour. Place the dough in a lightly oiled bowl. Turn to coat with oil. Cover with cling film (plastic wrap). Set aside in a warm place for 1 hour, or until doubled in size.
2. Knead the dough, working in the mixed fruit peel and raisins on a lightly floured surface. Roll into a log. Cut into 18 even-sized pieces. Shape the pieces into buns.
3. Place the buns, 2.5 cm (1 in) apart on greased baking trays. Cover and set aside in a warm place for 20 minutes.
4. For the cross, place the flour and 75 ml (2½ fl oz/¹/₃ cup) water in a bowl. Beat until smooth. Spoon into a piping bag fitted with a small plain nozzle. Mark a cross on top of each bun.
5. Preheat the oven to 200°C/400°F/Gas mark 6. Bake for 15 minutes, or until golden.
6. For the glaze, mix all the remaining ingredients until smooth. Brush over the warm buns.

makes 18

Soda bread

160 g (5½ oz/1¹/₃ cups) plain (all-purpose) flour, plus extra for dusting
1 teaspoon bicarbonate of soda (baking soda)
1 teaspoon salt
45 g (1½ oz) butter, plus extra for greasing
500 ml (17 fl oz/2 cups) buttermilk or milk

1. Preheat oven to 200°C/400°F/Gas mark 6.
2. Sift the flour, baking soda and salt into a bowl. Rub in the butter, using your fingertips, until the mixture resembles coarse breadcrumbs. Make a well in the centre of the flour mixture, pour in the milk or buttermilk and, using a round-ended knife, mix to form a soft dough.
3. Turn the dough onto a floured surface and knead lightly until smooth. Shape into an 18 cm/7 in round, and place on a greased and floured baking tray. Score the dough into eighths using a sharp knife. Dust lightly with flour and bake for 35–40 minutes, or until the loaf sounds hollow when tapped on the base.

serves 8

Country cornbread

115 g (4 oz / 1 cup) cornmeal
115 g (4 oz / 1 cup) plain (all-purpose) flour
2 tablespoons sugar
1 tablespoon baking powder
½ teaspoon salt
175 ml (6 fl oz / ¾ cup) milk
125 ml (4 fl oz / ½ cup) sour cream
2 eggs
100 g (3½ oz) butter, melted

1. Preheat the oven to 180°C/350°F/Gas mark 4. Grease and line a 9 x 9 in (23 x 23 cm) square cake tin (pan).
2. In a large mixing bowl, stir together all the dry ingredients. In another bowl, mix the milk, cream, eggs and butter together well. Pour into the flour mixture and mix until just combined.
3. Pour the batter into a the prepared tin. Bake for approximately 30 minutes, or until a skewer inserted into the bread comes out clean. Cut into squares or rectangles and serve warm.

serves 8

Banana bread

115 g (4 oz / ½ cup) butter, at room temperature, plus extra for greasing and serving
200 g (7 oz / 1 cup) caster (superfine) sugar
2 eggs, lightly beaten
3 ripe bananas, peeled
2 tablespoons honey
2 tablespoons lemon juice
1 teaspoon vanilla extract
175 g (6 oz / 1½ cups) self-raising (self-rising) flour, sifted
½ teaspoon baking soda
1 teaspoon ground cinnamon
55 g (2 oz / ½ cup) almond meal (ground almonds)

1. Preheat oven to 180°C/350°F/Gas mark 4. Lightly grease a 23 x 15 cm/9 x 6 in loaf tin (pan).
2. In a mixing bowl, beat the butter and sugar until light and creamy using an electric beater. Add the eggs and beat until combined.
3. In a food processor, combine the bananas, honey, lemon juice and vanilla until smooth.
4. Stir the banana mixture into the butter and sugar mixture and stir until well combined. Gently fold in the flour, baking soda, cinnamon and almond meal.
5. Spoon the batter into prepared tin and bake for 50–60 minutes, or until cooked. Leave to cool for 5 minutes then turn out onto a wire rack.
6. Cut into slices and serve with butter or place under a grill (broiler) and serve hot.

serves 8

Traditional scones (biscuits)

225 g (8 oz/2 cups) self-raising (self-rising) flour, plus extra for dusting
1 teaspoon baking powder
2 teaspoons sugar
45 g (1½ oz) butter, plus extra for greasing
1 egg
125 ml (4 fl oz/½ cup) milk
strawberry preserve and whipped cream, to serve

1. Preheat the oven to 220°C/425°F/Gas mark 7.
2. Sift together the flour and baking powder into a large bowl. Stir in the sugar, then rub in the butter using your fingertips, until the mixture resembles coarse breadcrumbs.
3. In another bowl, whisk together the egg and milk. Make a well in the centre of the flour mixture, pour in the egg mixture and mix to form a soft dough. Turn onto a lightly floured surface and knead lightly.
4. Press the dough out to a 2 cm (¾ in) thickness, using the palm of your hand. Cut out the scones using a floured 5 cm (2 in) cookie cutter. Avoid twisting the cutter, or the scones will rise unevenly.
5. Arrange the scones close together on a greased and lightly floured baking sheet. Brush with a little milk and bake for 12–15 minutes, or until golden. Serve with strawberry preserve and whipped cream.

makes 12

Honey scones (biscuits)

450 g (1 lb/4 cups) self-raising (self-rising) flour, plus extra for dusting
1 teaspoon salt
55 g (2 oz) butter, plus extra for greasing
1 egg
2 tablespoons honey
grated zest of 1 orange
350 ml (12 fl oz/1½ cups) milk
1 egg beaten with 60 ml (2 fl oz/¼ cup) milk, to glaze
butter, to serve

1. Preheat the oven to 230°C/450°F/Gas mark 8. Grease and dust a baking sheet with flour.
2. Sift the flours and salt into a large bowl then, using your fingertips, rub the butter into the flour mixture. Add the egg, honey and zest. Make a well in the centre and add the milk all at once, stirring quickly and lightly to a soft dough.
3. Turn out onto a lightly floured surface and knead just enough to make a smooth surface. Roll out to 2 cm (¾ in) thick. Stamp out rounds using a 5 cm (2 in) cookie cutter.
4. Arrange on the baking sheet. Brush the tops with the combined beaten egg and milk and then bake for 10 minutes, or until golden.

makes 12–16

Strawberry preserve

2 kg (4 lb 6 oz) granulated (white) sugar
2 kg (4 lb 6 oz) strawberries, hulled
juice and zest of 2 lemons

1. Set the oven temperature to 140°C/275°F/Gas mark 1. Put the sugar in an ovenproof pan and place in the oven.
2. Put the strawberries and lemon in a saucepan and heat gently, stirring as the juice begins to flow out of the fruit. When the juice is coming to the boil, add the warmed sugar.
3. After it has dissolved, bring the preserve to a rapid boil until it thickens and reaches the setting point (about 15–20 minutes).
4. Remove from the heat and let stand for 15 minutes. Ladle into sterilised jars, label and seal.

Note: A perennial favourite, strawberry jelly or jam tastes delicious with warm fresh croissants and tea.

makes 4 kg/8 lb 13 oz

Dry fig preserve

1 kg (2¼ lb) dried figs, roughly chopped
2 litres (3½ pints/8 cups) water
2 lemons
1 teaspoon fennel seeds
3 tablespoons pine nuts
55 g (2 oz) flaked almonds
725 g (1 lb 10 oz) granulated (white) sugar

1. Soak the dried figs in 1 litre/1¾ pints of water for several hours.
2. Put the lemon zest and pips into a muslin bag. Squeeze the lemon juice (retaining the pips and zest) into the soaked figs with the rest of the water. Put the bag of zest and pips in a saucepan and bring to the boil. Simmer until the figs are tender, stirring constantly.
3. Add the fennel seeds, pine nuts, flaked almonds and sugar, then stir until the sugar dissolves. Squeeze the juice out of the muslin bag into the mixture and discard the bag. Boil, stirring constantly, until the setting point is reached.
4. Ladle the preserve into warm sterilized jars. Label and seal.

Note: This dried fig preserve is very easy to make. It tastes delicious and is very rich.

makes 3.5 kg (7 lb 12 oz)

Baked eggs

100 g (3½ oz) spinach leaves, coarsely chopped
50 g (1¼ oz) salted ricotta, sliced
60 ml (2 fl oz / ¼ cup) double (heavy / thickened) cream
2 large eggs

1. Preheat the oven to 190°C/375°F/Gas mark 5.
2. Place two ramekins in a deep baking tray.
3. Wash the spinach and cook in a medium pan set over low heat until wilted. Drain the excess water. Transfer the spinach to a medium bowl. Add the ricotta and cream and stir to combine. Spoon the spinach mixture into the ramekins then break an egg into the centre.
4. Fill the baking tray with boiling water to come halfway up the sides of the ramekins. Bake in the oven for 15 minutes, or until the eggs have set.

serves 2

Poached eggs on toast

1. Bring a medium saucepan of water to the simmer. Using a spoon, create a whirlpool and crack the eggs one at a time into the centre. Poach for about 3 minutes or until the whites are slightly firm.
2. Toast the bread in a toaster until golden brown. Arrange the toast, eggs, rocket and chutney onto two serving plates.

serves 2

Eggs Benedict

8 English muffins, toasted
2 tablespoons butter, softened
8 thin slices ham
8 poached eggs
1 tablespoon caviar
1 lime, cut into wedges

FOR THE HOLLANDAISE SAUCE
115 g (4 oz) butter
4 egg yolks
1½ tablespoons lemon juice
salt and freshly ground black pepper

1. To make the Hollandaise sauce, cut the butter into thirds. Place the egg yolks and one-third of the butter in a heatproof bowl and set it over a pan over simmering, but not boiling, water until the butter melts, stirring quickly.
2. Add the next third of butter, still stirring. The mixture will start to thicken, then add the last third of butter. When the butter is melted, remove the pan from the hot water and stir quickly for about 2 minutes. Stir in the lemon juice, a teaspoon at a time, then add the salt and pepper.
3. Heat again over hot water, stirring constantly. When heated, remove immediately.
4. Spread the toast with a little butter, then top each piece with a slice of ham, a poached egg and Hollandaise sauce. Serve with a little caviar on top and a wedge of lime.

serves 4

Fried eggs with bacon

1 tablespoon butter
8 eggs
8 rashers (strips) bacon
4 tomatoes, sliced

1. Heat a large non-stick frying pan. Add the bacon and fry until some fat is released into the pan. Add the tomatoes and continue cooking until golden brown on both sides.
2. Heat the butter in another frying pan set over a low heat. Crack the eggs into a bowl and slide the eggs gently into the pan. Cover the pan and cook for 1 minute, take off the lid and baste the eggs with butter, then replace the lid for about 2 minutes, or until white is firm. If your frying pan has no lid just baste with the butter until desired consistency.
3. Serve eggs with bacon and tomatoes.

serves 4

Breakfast feast

8 rashers (strips) bacon
4 tomatoes, halved
2 onions, thinly sliced
4 lean sausages
2 teaspoons white vinegar
1 tablespoon plain (all-purpose) flour
salt and freshly ground black pepper
8 large eggs, at room temperature
4 slices Turkish bread, toasted

1. Dry-fry the bacon and tomato pieces in a non-stick frying pan, then transfer to plate and place in a warm oven. Fry the onions in the same pan with the sausages. Cook for 8 minutes, turning a few times.
2. Sprinkle the flour over the sausages and onion, stirring well. Add 125 ml (4 fl oz/½ cup) of hot water and salt and pepper to taste. Cover and simmer for 5 minutes.
3. Meanwhile, half-fill a separate large frying pan with water and bring to a simmer. Add the vinegar.
4. Swirl the simmering frying pan with a large spoon to create a gentle whirlpool motion. Crack the eggs into the centre of the water and gently swirl the water again. After the water returns to the simmer, wait 2 minutes longer and gently remove and drain the poached eggs. Serve the eggs on top of the Turkish bread with the bacon, tomato, sauage and onion at the side.

serves 4

Scrambled eggs

8 eggs
150 ml (5 fl oz /⅔ cup) milk
salt and freshly ground black pepper
30 g (1 oz) butter

1. In a bowl, beat the eggs lightly then add the milk, salt and pepper.
2. Heat the butter in a frying pan set over a gentle heat, add the beaten eggs and stir
    continuously with a wooden spoon until a creamy texture.

Note: Scrambled eggs can become a gourmet meal with imaginative additives such as:
• Chopped chives or parsley and crisp bacon crumbles
• Sliced mushrooms, previously fried in butter
• Skinned and grilled (broiled) tomato, chopped finely
• Finely grated orange zest
• Dice cooked potatoes, fried to golden brown
• Anchovies soaked in milk, drained, and sliced.

serves 4

Omelette

2 eggs
freshly ground black pepper
1 tablespoon butter

1. Place the eggs, 2 tablespoons of water and black pepper, to taste, in a bowl, and whisk lightly to combine.
2. Heat an omelette pan over a medium heat until hot. Add butter, tipping the pan so the base is completely coated. Heat until the butter is foaming, but not browned, then add the egg mixture. As it sets, use a palette knife or fork to gently draw up the edge of the omelette until no liquid remains and the omelette is lightly set.
3. Serve the omelette plain, or topped with filling of your choice, and fold in half. Slip omelette onto a plate and serve immediately.

serves 1

SOUP

Soup

What is soup? What's the difference between a broth, a chowder, a boullabaisse, a consommé, a bisque and a vichyssoise? The dish of soup must be as old as time. Maybe the first made wouldn't be recognisable today, but any dish that could be cooked in just one pot must have been popular from the cook's point of view. Historically a soup was water boiled with the addition of whatever ingredients were to hand. The inclusion of vegetables or grains would add bulk as well as flavour. A clever cook would use up leftover ingredients in a soup, eking out scarce ingredients, or adding herbs and spices to mask as well as add flavour. Soup could be the food of the rich man or the pauper and almost any ingredient could be added to it.

Today we associate chicken soup with food for the invalid; a dish made with the goodness from the roasted bones of the chicken carcass and combined with herbs, milk or stock and other flavourings to create a concoction that isn't too rich, but is easy to eat, smells divine and will offer nourishment in a drinkable package. It's a food type that children adore for the same reason, though often their preferred varieties come straight from the can.

Every culture is known for a particular type of soup: in China, there's the wonton soup, in France, the French onion; in Italy there's minestrone, made with locally produced pasta; in Spain, there's the boullabaisse, a hearty stew-like concoction that incorporates local seafood. Today we have access to such a broad base of ingredients all year round that we can make any soup our heart desires. So, whether your choice is for a clear and intensely flavoured consommé, a thin broth with hints of ingredient added, a thickened purée of grains and vegetables, a luxurious and richly flavoured dish with the addition of cream, or any of the stew-like combinations, there's sure to be a recipe here that you will love, as well as others that inspire your culinary creations.

From childhood favourites to sophisticated adult dishes, there are recipes here that will fit any mealtime and pander to any taste. For those who love the old-fashioned dishes, there are recipes for traditional pea and ham, and oxtail soups. For children and those who cling to their child's palate, recipes are provided for tomato, and for chicken soup. For winter-warming dishes there is lamb shank broth, and hearty beef and barley soup. If you're entertaining then you might like to try the seafood bisque. Each recipe represents a dish suitable to serve as an entire meal. Of course, you can add breads of all varieties, cheese scones and even salads to add more sustenance, or keep it light and serve a small helping as a precursor to a main course.

Pumpkin soup

1.5 kg (3 lb 5 oz) pumpkin, peeled and cut into large cubes
2 tomatoes, chopped
1 large onion, chopped
1.25 litres (2¼ pints / 5 cups) vegetable stock
pinch of salt
pinch of cayenne pepper
150 ml (5 fl oz / ⅔ cup double (heavy / thickened) cream
2 tablespoons (¼ cup) flat-leaf parsley, finely chopped

1. Combine the pumpkin flesh, tomato and onions with the stock in a pan. Simmer gently until the pumpkin is tender, approximately 20 minutes.
2. Purée the pumpkin mixture. Return to the pan, add the salt, cayenne pepper and cream and reheat gently.
3. Serve sprinkled with parsley.

serves 6

Cream of chicken soup

55 g (2 oz) butter
4 tablespoons plain (all-purpose) flour
1.25 litres (2¼ pints / 5 cups) chicken stock (see recipe)
600 ml (1 pint) scalded milk (or ½ milk and ½ cream)
1 chicken breast, shredded
1 small stalk celery, finely chopped
few drops Tabasco sauce
salt and freshly ground black pepper, to taste
2 egg yolks
fresh chives, chopped, to serve

1. Melt the butter in a large saucepan, stir in the flour and cook for about 1 minute, then add the half the chicken stock. Stir continuously over medium heat until boiling. Add the remaining stock, milk, chicken, celery, Tabasco sauce and salt and pepper, and bring to the boil. Reduce the heat and simmer, covered, for 5 minutes.
2. In a bowl, beat the egg yolks well with a fork, then pour into a heated tureen. Pour the soup very slowly over the egg yolks, stirring all the time with a wooden spoon.
3. Scatter with some fresh chives. Serve immediately.

serves 4

Cream of mushroom soup

225 g (8 oz) mushrooms
115 g (4 oz) butter
½ teaspoon salt
freshly ground black pepper, to taste
3 garlic cloves, finely chopped
1.25 litres (2¼ pints / 5 cups) chicken stock (see recipe)
125 ml (4 fl oz / ½ cup) fresh cream, at room temperature
garlic-flavoured croutons, for serving
parsley, chopped, to serve

1. Select some of the smallest mushrooms and take a slice from the centre of each. Set aside for the garnish.
2. Wipe the mushrooms with a damp kitchen towel (do not peel them) and thinly slice them. In a frying pan, heat the butter to sizzling, then fry the mushrooms with salt and a good grind of black pepper. Set aside to cool, then purée in a blender or food processor with the garlic and 250 ml (8 fl oz / 1 cup) of the stock.
3. Pour the remaining stock into a large saucepan. Add the purée and heat the soup to simmering point. Stir in the cream. Add the reserved mushroom slices and simmer for 5 minutes. Taste and adjust the seasoning if necessary.
4. Serve hot with garlic-flavoured croutons and a scattering of parsley.

serves 4

Pea soup

250 g (9 oz) split peas
500 g (1 lb 2 oz) bacon bones
2 carrots, roughly chopped
2 turnips, roughly chopped
2 onions, roughly chopped
4 stalks celery, chopped
salt and freshly ground
black pepper
1 tablespoon plain (all-purpose) flour, mixed with 1 tablespoon water

1. Wash the peas and soak them in water overnight. Place the peas, water and bones in a saucepan and bring to the boil. Add the prepared vegetables and simmer gently for 1½ hours.
2. Remove the bones, purée the mixture, and season with salt and pepper. Thicken with flour paste and, stir continuously, cooking for 3 minutes. Garnish with croutons and serve immediately.

serves 8

Tomato soup

750 g (1 lb 10 oz) ripe tomatoes, chopped
1 potato, peeled and chopped
1 small onion, chopped
1 sprig fresh basil
1 teaspoon sugar
2 tablespoons tomato paste
salt and freshly ground black pepper
250 ml (8 fl oz / 1 cup) vegetable stock
60 ml (2 fl oz / ¼ cup) double (heavy / thickened) cream
2 tablespoons (¼ cup) parsley, finely chopped

1. Place all the ingredients except for the parsley and cream into a saucepan with the stock. Bring to the boil and simmer, covered, for 20 minutes.
2. Serve the soup with a swirl of cream and scatter with chopped parsley.

serves 4

Oxtail soup

1 oxtail
1 tablespoon seasoned plain (all-purpose) flour
2 tablespoons oil
1.5 litres (2¾ pints / 6 cups) beef stock
1 carrot, sliced
1 small turnip, sliced
1 onion, roughly chopped
2 stalks celery, chopped
2–3 bay leaves
salt
pinch of cayenne pepper
juice of 1 lemon
1 teaspoon Worcestershire sauce
3 tablespoons sherry or Madeira

1. Coat the oxtail in seasoned flour. Heat the oil over a medium heat, add the oxtail and cook until brown. Add the stock and simmer for 2 hours. Skim off the froth.
2. Place the vegetables and bay leaves in the stock and cook for another 15–20 minutes.
3. Remove the meat from the bones, return the meat to the soup and reheat. Season with salt and cayenne pepper. Stir in the lemon juice and Worcestershire sauce. Just before serving, add the sherry.

serves 8

Chicken soup with dumplings

2 tablespoons vegetable oil	

2 tablespoons vegetable oil

3 large onions, chopped

3 large carrots, chopped

4 stalks celery, chopped

2 kg (4 lb 6 oz) chicken wings, or chicken pieces

4 bay leaves

6 sprigs parsley, plus extra to serve

300 g (10½ oz) beef top rib

For the matzo balls

2 tablespoons vegetable oil

1 large onion, finely diced

4 large eggs

¼ small bunch chives, chopped

60–90 g (2–3 oz / 1–1½ cups) matzo meal

salt and freshly ground black pepper

1. To make the soup, heat the oil in a very large saucepan and add the onions, carrots and celery and sauté in the oil until golden, about 10 minutes. Add the chicken, bay leaves, parsley, top rib and 4 litres (7 pints) of water and bring to the boil. Simmer for 5 hours, skimming the scum off the surface as it becomes visible. After 5 hours, taste the soup and season to taste. Leave to go cold, then chill the soup overnight. The next day, skim the fat off the surface of the soup then reheat until just warm. Strain the soup into a clean pan, discarding the solids.

2. To make the matzo balls, heat the vegetable oil in a frying pan and add the finely chopped onions. Sauté until the onions are deep golden brown. Remove the pan from the heat and add the eggs, chives, matzo meal and salt and pepper to taste and mix thoroughly. Allow the mixture to chill for 2 hours. Bring a large pan of salted water to the boil and then shape the matzo mixture into walnut-size balls and drop them into the boiling water. Simmer for approximately 30 minutes, or until tender. Remove with a slotted spoon and set aside.

3. To serve, reheat the soup until scalding then add the matzo balls to heat them through. Serve 1–2 matzo balls per person with a bowl of soup and garnish with parsley.

serves 10

Minestrone

75 ml (2½ fl oz / ¹/3 cup) olive oil
1 medium brown onion, sliced
1 garlic clove, crushed
250 g (9 oz) potatoes, peeled and chopped
150 g (5 oz) carrots, thinly sliced
115 g (4 oz) celery, thinly sliced
150 g (5 oz) courgette (zucchini), sliced
1 litre (1¾ pints / 4 cups) vegetable stock
400 g (14 oz) can tomatoes
rind from piece of Parmesan
2 tablespoons (¼ cup) parsley, chopped
400 g (14 oz) can cannellini beans
salt and freshly ground black pepper

1. Heat the oil in a large pan and cook the onion and garlic for 5 minutes until the onion is tender. Add the potatoes and cook for another 5 minutes. Repeat with the carrots, celery and courgette.
2. Add the beef stock, tomatoes and cheese rind, bring to the boil and simmer covered for 1 hour. If the soup becomes too thick, add more stock.
3. Add the chopped parsley and cannellini beans, and heat for another 10 minutes.
4. To serve, remove the cheese rind, season with salt and black pepper, and serve with crusty bread.

serves 6

French onion soup

50 g (1¾ oz) butter
600 g (1¼ lb) onions, peeled and sliced
2 litres (3½ pints / 8 cups) beef stock
2 tablespoons (¼ cup) parsley, chopped
1 teaspoon salt
generous pinch of cayenne pepper
nutmeg, to taste
3 egg yolks
60 ml (2 fl oz / ¼ cup) port

1. Melt the butter in a deep heavy pan and add the onions when the butter is foaming. Fry the onions until dark brown without burning, stirring constantly.
2. Add the stock and bring to the boil. Boil for 45 minutes and then add the parsley, salt and cayenne pepper and nutmeg. Return to the boil and cook for another 10 minutes.
3. To serve, pour the soup into a tureen and keep hot.
4. Mix the egg yolks with the port in a sauceboat. Pour the egg yolk mixture into the soup while stirring and serve immediately with crusty bread.

serves 6

Pea and ham soup

500 g (1 lb 2 oz) dried split peas
1 kg (2¼ lb) bacon bones
2.5 litres (4 pints / 10 cups) chicken stock
2 frankfurters
2 teaspoons white vinegar
sliced sour gherkins, to garnish

1. Soak the peas overnight. Drain and rinse. Add the peas and bacon bones to the stock in a large pot. Bring to the boil and simmer for 2½ hours. Leave to cool and remove the bacon bones. Scrape the meat off the bones and return the meat to the soup.
2. Cook the frankfurters in boiling water for 3 minutes. Leave to cool, then peel them and cut them into 5 mm (¼ in) slices. Add to the soup with the white vinegar. Reheat the soup and serve with sour gherkins.

serves 8

Hearty beef and barley soup

40 g (1¼ oz / ⅓ cup) wholemeal (whole-wheat) flour
1 teaspoon salt
500 g (1 lb 2 oz) lean stewing beef
2 tablespoons olive oil
1 medium onion, chopped
4 large garlic cloves, minced
½ medium carrot, grated (shredded)
1 stalk celery, chopped
1 large tomato, diced
175 g (6 oz / 1 cup) barley
1.25 litres (2¼ pints / 5 cups) chicken stock
2 tablespoons (¼ cup) basil, chopped
1 bay leaf
salt and freshly ground black pepper

1. In a plastic bag, combine the flour, salt and meat. Shake vigorously.
2. Heat the oil in a large saucepan over medium heat and quickly brown the meat. Add onions and garlic and cook until soft, about 3–4 minutes. Add the carrot, celery and tomato and continue cooking for about 5 minutes.
3. Add the barley, stock and basil and bring to the boil. Wrap the bay leaf in muslin and add to the pot. Lower the heat and allow to simmer until the barley is soft, about 20–25 minutes.
4. Season to taste with the salt and pepper. Remove the bay leaf before serving.

serves 8

Chicken and corn soup

1¼ kg (2 lb 12 oz) chicken
55 g (2 oz / ½ cup) water chestnuts, drained
1 small onion, peeled and halved
2 rashers (strips) bacon, each rasher cut into quarters,
rind removed
0.5 cm (¼ in) piece green ginger, peeled
425 g (15 oz) can corn niblets, drained,
liquid reserved

6 spring onions (scallions), sliced
2 teaspoons sesame oil
salt and freshly ground black pepper
3 tablespoons cornflour (corn starch)
1 tablespoon sweet sherry
2 teaspoons soy sauce
1 egg

1. Wash the chicken and place it into a large saucepan with 2.5 litres (4¼ pints/10 cups) water. Bring to the boil and simmer for approximately 40 minutes, or until the chicken is cooked. Remove the chicken from the pan, and set aside to cool, retaining the chicken stock.
2. Meanwhile, place the water chestnuts, onion, bacon and ginger into a food processor or blender bowl and process until finely chopped. Remove from the bowl.
3. Purée the corn niblets in a food processor or blender.
4. Remove the skin and bones from the chicken. Place the chicken into the processor bowl and process until finely chopped.
5. Take 500 ml (17 fl oz/2 cups) of chicken stock from the pan and reserve for future use.
6. Add all the prepared ingredients with the reserved corn liquid to the chicken stock.
7. Add the spring onions to the pan with the sesame oil, salt and pepper. Bring to the boil. Mix the cornflour with 75 ml (2½ fl oz/⅓cup) water to a smooth paste, add to the soup and simmer, stirring, for 3 minutes. Add the sherry and soy sauce. Lightly beat the egg with a fork, add to the soup and stir for 1 minute. Serve.

serves 12

Lamb shank broth

30 g (1 oz) butter
1 large onion, sliced
4 lamb shanks
90 g (3 oz / ½ cup) barley
3 celery stalks, sliced
2 large carrots, sliced
2 large parsnips, diced
2 tomatoes, diced
1 teaspoon salt
freshly ground black pepper
2 tablespoons (¼ cup) parsley, chopped

1. Melt the butter in a large stockpot. Add the onion and cook over a low heat for 10 minutes. Add the shanks, barley, celery, carrots, parsnips, tomatoes and 3 litres (4¼ pints/12 cups) water. Season with salt and pepper. Cover and simmer for 1½–2 hours.
2. Remove the lamb shanks and chop the meat. Return the meat to the soup and discard the bones. Adjust the seasoning, if necessary.
3. Serve sprinkled with parsley and accompanied with wholemeal (whole-wheat) crusty bread rolls.

serves 8

Seafood bisque

90 g (3 oz) butter

1 small onion, diced

1 garlic clove, crushed

1 small carrot, diced

1 celery stalk, sliced

750 ml (24 fl oz/3 cups) fish stock

2 tablespoons lemon juice

1 bay leaf

1 sprig thyme, leaves removed and stalks discarded

¼ teaspoon Tabasco sauce

½ teaspoon Worcestershire sauce

250 ml (8 fl oz/1 cup) double (heavy/thickened) cream

1 kg (2¼ lb) seafood, finely diced

125 ml (4 fl oz/½ cup) dry white wine

1 lemon, thinly sliced

2 tablespoons (¼ cup) parsley, chopped

1. Melt the butter in a large stockpot set over medium heat and sauté the onion and garlic for 5 minutes. Add the carrot and celery and fry for another 3 minutes.
2. In a jug (pitcher), combine the fish stock, lemon juice, bay leaf, thyme, Tabasco and Worcestershire sauces, add to the pot and simmer for 30 minutes, or until tender.
3. Remove the bay leaf, purée the mixture, add the cream, seafood and wine and reheat without boiling. Garnish with lemon and parsley and serve.

serves 8

Rich vegetable stock

2 tablespoons olive oil
1 turnip or swede, peeled and chopped
5 cloves garlic, sliced
3 stalks celery, washed and sliced
3 large carrots, peeled and sliced
10 mushrooms, wiped and sliced
3 large onions, peeled and sliced

4 tomatoes, washed
2 leeks, well washed and sliced
2 parsnips, peeled and sliced
10 sprigs parsley, finely chopped
1 teaspoon peppercorns
8 Brussels sprouts, outer leaves removed
4 bay leaves

1. Heat the olive oil in a large stockpot and sauté all the vegetables for 20 minutes until they begin to develop a golden colour on the surface.
2. Add the parsley, peppercorns, bay leaves and water to cover (about 4 litres/7 pints) and bring to the boil. Simmer for 3 hours, skimming the surface to remove any scum that accumulates.
3. Add salt to taste, then simmer for a few more minutes if you would like a more intense flavour. Allow to cool then strain, pressing on the solids. Use within three days, or freeze for up to 12 months.

Note: In addition to the vegetables above, you can add any other vegetables in your refrigerator that are past their prime – greens, root vegetables, corn and bell peppers all work well.

makes 2 litres (3½ pints)

Chicken stock

2 carrots

4 stalks celery

3 onions

1 leek, chopped

8 sprigs parsley, chopped

2 kg (4 lb 6 oz) chicken carcasses or wings

1 teaspoon peppercorns

1. Wash all the vegetables and slice or chop roughly.
2. Place all the ingredients in a large stockpot. Add water to generously cover the ingredients (about 4 litres/7 pints). Bring to the boil, then simmer for 2–3 hours, skimming the scum off the surface as it rises to the top.
3. Add salt to taste, then strain the stock through a sieve lined with absorbent paper or muslin.
4. Place in a large saucepan and chill until the fat solidifies on the surface. Remove the fat and use or freeze the stock.

makes 2.5 litres (4½ pints)

Veal stock

1 kg (2¼ lb) veal breast or veal shin meat, cut into 7.5 cm (3 in) pieces

2 kg (4 lb 6 oz) veal bones (preferably knuckles), cracked

2 carrots

4 celery stalks

3 onions

4 sprigs fresh thyme, leaves removed and stalks discarded

3 unpeeled cloves garlic, crushed

8 black peppercorns

1 bay leaf

salt

1. Fill a large stockpot halfway with water. Bring the water to the boil, add the veal meat and bones, and blanch them for 2 minutes to clean them.
2. Drain the meat and bones in a colander, and discard the liquid. Rinse the meat and bones under cold running water and return them to the pot.
3. Wash all the vegetables and slice or chop roughly them. Put them in a large stockpot with the veal bones and meat and all the remaining ingredients.
4. Cover with cold water (about 4 litres/7 pints), bring to the boil and simmer for 2–3 hours, skimming the scum off the surface as it rises to the top.
5. Add salt to taste, then strain through a sieve lined with absorbent paper or muslin.
6. Place in a large pan and chill until the fat solidifies on the surface. Remove the fat and use or freeze the stock.

makes 2.5 litres (4½ pints)

Fish stock

500 g (1 lb 2 oz) fish bones, heads and trimmings, washed
2 carrots, chopped
4 stalks celery, chopped
3 onions, roughly chopped
8 sprigs parsley, chopped
6 white peppercorns
generous pinch of ground nutmeg
1 teaspoon salt

1. Place the fish pieces and 1 litre (1¾ pints/4 cups) water into a large pan and bring to the boil.
2. Skim off any discoloured froth from the top. Add the remaining ingredients and simmer gently, uncovered, for another 30 minutes. If cooked for too long the stock becomes bitter.
3. Strain and discard the bones and vegetables. Use the stock within 2 days or freeze it in a sealed container.

makes 2.5 litres (10 cups)

Seafood stock

1 kg (2¼ lb) shrimp (prawn) shells and heads

2 carrots

4 stalks celery

3 onions

1 leek

8 sprigs parsley, chopped

1 teaspoon peppercorns

1. Thoroughly wash the shrimp shells and heads.
2. Wash all the vegetables and slice or chop roughly them, then place them in a large stockpot with the shells, parsley and peppercorns. Cover with cold water (about 4 litres/7 pints), bring to the boil and simmer for 1–2 hours, skimming the scum off the surface as it rises to the top.
3. Add salt to taste, then strain through a sieve lined with absorbent paper or muslin.
4. Place in a large saucepan and chill until the fat solidifies on the surface. Remove the fat and use or freeze the stock.

makes 1 litre (1¾ pints/4 cups)

MAIN COURSES

Main courses

No book of classic recipes would be complete without a chapter that included the world's most popular main course dishes. From childhood favourites, to stews, pies, roasts and pasta dishes, this chapter contains all the dishes that we love to eat.

Who can resist the Sunday roast? Whether your penchant is for lamb, beef, pork, chicken or turkey, these are the dishes that bring families and friends together. A roast is a highlight in the culinary calendar. It takes time to plan a roast dinner and all the accompaniments, as well as to shop for it. The preparation might begin the evening before the meal is due to be served, and all family members might be roped in to help with different tasks from peeling the vegetables, to testing to see if the meat is cooked. This is a meal that demands respect, both from the cook who creates it with skill, delivering every aspect piping hot to the table, each element ready to eat at the same time, as well as from the diners, who enjoy the anticipation of the feast as much as the event itself. There's an element of pressure about cooking a roast. The meat especially represents a sizeable investment of the weekly shopping budget. It has to taste good, and the cook has to make the best of the cut purchased. If you're feeding large numbers then there can be no mistakes. Expectation is high. It is at such meals that memories are made.

In this chapter, we understand the pressures created by cooking a roast dinner and provide you with clear step-by-step instructions for preparing the meat, as well as the cooking of it and there is plenty of information provided to make sure the entire meal is all timed to perfection. Of course, practice makes perfect and cooking confidence comes with having a few successes under your belt.

If you're a novice, start by cooking dishes that sre difficult to spoil. Childhood favourites such as cottage pie and spaghetti Bolognese will withstand extra cooking time, if you haven't got the timing just right. Alternatively, some dishes benefit from long slow cooking times, so once the dish is underway you only need to worry about the accompaniment that you will serve. Everyday meals generally involve cheaper cuts of meat as well as smaller quantities of produce. The advantage is two-fold: it's easier to check that the meat is cooked through and though the cooking time is shorter, because these cuts are less expensive, you can afford to make them more often and with each attempt, your confidence will soar.

The everyday meals included, incorporate fish dishes, pasta dishes and pies. Who doesn't love a pie? Whether it's encased or topped with pastry or potato, pies are a staple in many family homes.

Mostly they're associated with colder months, but included here is a recipe for quiche, which can be eaten hot and served with vegetables, then if there are leftovers, it can be eaten cold with salad for an easy lunch.

For quick and easy meals why not serve up pasta dishes? Just make batches of sauce and freeze it in portions, then you really will have meals in minutes.

Roast beef with gravy

1.5 kg (3 lb) rolled sirloin of beef
salt and freshly ground black pepper, to taste
butter or olive oil, for roasting

FOR THE GRAVY

pan juices from the roast meat
2–3 tablespoons plain (all-purpose) flour
500 ml (17 fl oz/2 cups) beef stock (see recipe), or water
salt and pepper, to taste

1. Preheat the oven to 160°C/325°F/Gas mark 3. Rub the meat with salt and pepper and place in a roasting pan, fat side up. If the joint has little fat, add 1–2 tablespoons butter or oil to the pan. Put the beef in the oven and cook for 2 hours.
2. Remove the roast beef to a hot carving platter and leave to stand in a warm place for 15–30 minutes before carving. This makes it easier to carve the meat.
3. Meanwhile, to make the gravy: after removing the roast from the baking tray, leave about 250 ml (8 fl oz/1 cup) of pan juices to make the gravy.
4. Place the tray on the stovetop, set over a medium heat, and sprinkle the flour over the pan juices. Stir with a wooden spoon until the mixture thickens. Add the stock, stirring constantly, and simmer gently for 5–10 minutes. Add a little extra stock or water, if necessary. Season with salt or pepper.

serves 6

Roast chicken

1. Preheat the oven to 180°C/350°F/Gas mark 4. Rub the chicken with salt, pepper and half the olive oil. Truss the chicken and place it in a greased roasting pan with the remaining oil. Cook in the oven, basting occasionally, for 1 hour, or until tender and golden brown all over. Remove the chicken and keep warm. While the chicken is cooking make the chicken stock.
2. Add the chicken stock to the pan juices and bring to the boil. Strain into a sauceboat and serve with the chicken, roast potatoes and green vegetables.

serves 6

Leg of lamb with vegetables

1 leg of lamb (about 1½ kg/3 lb 5 oz)
2 garlic cloves, cut into slivers
2 fresh rosemary sprigs, cut into small pieces
salt and black pepper
400 g (14 oz) parsnips, chopped
300 g (10½ oz) carrots, chopped
6 heads chicory (curly endive) cut into quarters lengthwise
310 ml (10 fl oz/1¼ cups) red wine
2 tablespoons red wine vinegar

1. Preheat the oven to 350°F/180°C/Gas mark 4. Make several incisions in the lamb using a sharp knife. Push the garlic slivers and pieces of rosemary into the incisions, then season well.
2. Arrange the parsnips, carrots and chicory in a large roasting pan and place the lamb on top. Pour in the wine and vinegar and roast for 2–2½ hours until the lamb is tender, basting the lamb and turning the vegetables in the cooking juices every 30 minutes. Add a little more wine or water, if necessary.
3. Transfer the lamb to a plate, reserving the cooking juices, then cover with foil and rest for 15 minutes. Carve the lamb and serve with the vegetables, with the cooking juices drizzled over.

serves 4

Roast pork with apple sauce

3 kg (6½ lb) pork loin
salt, to taste
apple sauce, to serve

FOR THE APPLE SAUCE
4 large cooking apples, peeled and sliced
2 tablespoons caster (superfine) sugar
3 cloves
30 g (1 oz) butter

1. Preheat the oven to 240°C/475°F/Gas mark 9. Rub the pork with the salt and place in a roasting pan. Bake the pork in the oven for 30 minutes to crisp the crackling, then reduce the heat to 160°C/325°F/Gas mark 3 and cook for 3 hours. Continue to baste throughout the cooking time.
2. When the pork is cooked, place it in a carving tray and keep warm. Make gravy from the pan juices (see page 103).
3. Serve the roast pork with apple sauce, roast potatoes and roast vegetables.
4. To make the apple sauce: preheat the oven to 180°C/350°F/Gas mark 4. Put the apples in an ovenproof dish, sprinkle with sugar and cloves. Cover and place in the oven for about 30 minutes, or until the apples are soft. Remove the cloves, stir the apples until pulpy, then add butter in small pieces and leave to cool.

serves 8–12

Meatloaf

1 slice white bread
1 tablespoon milk
500 g (1 lb 2 oz) minced (ground) beef
3 tablespoons natural (plain) yogurt
30 g/1 oz French onion soup mix
½ teaspoon mixed dried herbs
45 g (1½ oz/½ cup) bran
3 spring onions (scallions), chopped
1 egg, beaten
freshly ground black pepper

1. Soak the bread in milk and squeeze dry. Mix thoroughly with all the remaining ingredients. Spoon into a greased cake tin (pan) and cover with a lid or foil.
2. Place the tin in a slow cooker and cook on low for approximately 4 hours or on high for approximately 3 hours. Serve hot or cold, with a green salad.

serves 4

Beer-glazed ham

16½ lb (7.5 kg) leg of ham
40 cloves
500 ml (17 fl oz/2 cups) stout, such as Guinness
225 g (8 oz/1 cup) soft brown sugar
2 tablespoons mustard
1 teaspoon ground ginger
2 teaspoons ground cardamom

1. Preheat the oven to 160°C/325°F/Gas mark 3. Remove the skin from the ham, leaving a portion of skin around the bone. Score the ham with diagonal lines in both directions and put a clove in the centre of each section.
2. Place the ham fat-side up in a roasting dish and pour over all but 4 tablespoons of the stout. Bake for 3 hours, basting occasionally with stout. Remove the ham from the oven and baste thoroughly.
3. Increase the oven temperature to 200°C/400°F/Gas mark 6. Combine the sugar, mustard, ginger, cardamom and enough remaining stout to make a paste. Spread the mixture over the ham and bake for 35 minutes, or until well glazed.

serves 20–30

Roast pork with mustard herbs

60 g (2 oz) butter
2 teaspoons Dijon mustard
1 teaspoon mixed herbs
2¾ lb (1.25 kg) piece of pork scotch fillet
1½ tablespoons olive oil
2 teaspoons honey

½ teaspoon ginger, ground
1 bunch baby carrots, peeled and trimmed
3 parsnips, peeled and cut into wedges
1 tablespoon plain (all-purpose) flour
375 ml (12 fl oz / 1½ cups) beef stock

1. Preheat the oven to 200°C/400°F/Gas mark 4.
2. Combine half the butter, the Dijon mustard and mixed herbs in a bowl. Spread the mixture over the pork roast.
3. Heat 2 teaspoons of oil in a large frying pan over high heat. Sear the meat quickly until light golden all over. Remove the meat, leaving the pan juices for gravy.
4. Wrap the meat in foil and place on a rack over a baking tray. Bake in the oven for 1¼–1½ hours or until cooked.
5. Meanwhile, heat the remaining oil and butter with the honey and ginger in a clean frying pan over low to medium heat. Sauté the carrots and parsnips for 10 minutes, turning from time to time.
6. To make the gravy, add the flour to the pan juices and cook over low heat. Add the beef stock and stir until the mixture is smooth and thickens.
7. Slice the meat and serve with sautéed carrots, parsnips and gravy.

serves 4

Braised steak

750 g / 1½ lb blade or topside steak, cut into four pieces
2 tablespoons plain (all-purpose) flour
60 g / 2 oz butter
1 brown onion, peeled and sliced
salt and freshly ground black pepper
250 ml (8 fl oz / 1 cup) beef stock
1 teaspoon Angostura bitters (optional)

1. Rub flour into each piece of steak on both sides.
2. Heat the butter in a frying pan, add the meat and brown quickly on both sides. Place meat in the slow cooker. Add sliced onion to the pan and sauté until golden brown.
3. Add the onion to the slow cooker with salt and pepper, stock and bitters, if using. Cook on low power in a slow cooker for 6–8 hours.

serves 4–5

Barbecued spare ribs

1 garlic clove, crushed
salt and black pepper, to taste
1 tablespoon brown sugar
1 teaspoon paprika
1 teaspoon dry mustard
8 pork spare ribs
barbecue sauce, for serving

1. In a bowl, combine the garlic, salt and pepper, sugar, paprika and mustard. Rub the spareribs with the seasoning.
2. Barbecue the spareribs over medium coals, turning frequently and basting with the barbecue sauce while cooking. Cook for 15–20 minutes, or until the spareribs are tender.
3. Serve with baked potatoes and coleslaw.

serves 8

Barbecued chicken drumsticks

12 chicken drumsticks

FOR THE MARINADE
60 ml (2 fl oz / ¼ cup) tomato sauce
2–3 tablespoons lemon juice
2 tablespoons soy sauce
60 ml (2 fl oz / ¼ cup) olive oil
½ teaspoon salt

1. To make the marinade, combine the ingredients in a large bowl and mix together well. Put the chicken drumsticks into the bowl, cover and leave to marinate.
2. Place the chicken on a grill (broiler) over medium hot coals or on a hot griddle set over medium heat and cook, turning regularly for 20 minutes, or until cooked through.

serves 6

Crumbed lamb cutlets

8 lamb cutlets
lemon juice, to taste (optional)
salt and freshly ground black pepper, to taste
plain (all-purpose) flour, for coating
1 egg, beaten with 1 tablespoon of water
breadcrumbs, for coating
olive oil, for frying
parsley, chopped, to garnish

1. Trim the skin and excess fat from the cutlets and flatten with the side of a meat mallet (unless it's already prepared this way). Arrange the cutlets on a plate, sprinkle with a little lemon juice (if using) and season with salt and pepper. Cover and refrigerate for 1 hour. To finish the cutlets, coat them with flour then dip in beaten egg and breadcrumbs, pressing them on firmly.
2. Fill a deep, heavy frying pan with oil to 5 mm (¼ in) deep and set over medium heat. Fry the cutlets for 4–5 minutes on each side, then transfer to a plate lined with absorbent paper.
3. Serve immediately, while crisp and piping hot, garnished with parsley.

Variations:
Parsley cutlets: to each 30 g (1 oz) breadcrumbs, add 2 tablespoons finely chopped parsley.
Parmesan cutlets: to each 30 g (1 oz) breadcrumbs, add 2 tablespoons grated Parmesan.
Rosemary cutlets: to each 30 g (1 oz) breadcrumbs, add ¼ teaspoon powdered or ½ teaspoon dried spikes of rosemary.

serves 4

Vienna schnitzel

500 g (1 lb 2 oz) veal steak, thinly cut from the leg
1 garlic clove, crushed (optional)
1 tablespoon lemon juice
salt and freshly ground black pepper, to taste
plain (all-purpose) flour, for coating

1 egg, beaten with 1 tablespoon water
breadcrumbs, for coating
olive oil, for frying
hard-boiled egg, anchovy fillets, capers, lemon slices
and parsley, to garnish

1. Flatten the veal between two pieces of plastic wrap (cling film), using the side of a meat mallet or rolling pin. Cut the skin on the edges to prevent curling during cooking. Arrange the veal on a plate and set aside.
2. Mix the garlic (optional) with lemon juice and brush onto the veal. Season with salt and pepper and allow to stand for 30 minutes. Dip each slice of veal into flour, then egg, and finally breadcrumbs, pressing them firmly on to coat the veal completely. Refrigerate for 1 hour.
3. Heat the oil in a frying pan and shallow fry the veal steaks over a moderate heat for about 2 minutes on each side, or until golden brown. Lift the veal onto absorbent paper to drain, then place on a hot serving platter.
4. Garnish each schnitzel with a slice of hard-boiled egg and top with a rolled anchovy fillet, a few capers, lemon slice and parsley.
5. Serve with boiled new potatoes, sauerkraut and a tossed salad.

serves 4

Beef casserole

1 tablespoon vegetable oil
1 kg (2¼ lb) blade steak, trimmed and cubed
2 onions, chopped
2 beef stock cubes, crumbled
2 carrots, sliced
1 parsnip, sliced
salt and freshly ground black pepper
1 bouquet garni
30 g / 1 oz butter
2 tablespoons plain (all-purpose) flour

1. Heat the oil in a frying pan. Pat the steak cubes dry with absorbent paper and brown them on all sides.
2. Add the onion to the pan and sauté until softened. Mix the stock cubes in 250 ml (8 fl oz/ 1 cup) hot water.
3. Place the stock, meat, onion, carrots, parsnip, salt and pepper and bouquet garni in a slow cooker. Cook for approximately 7–8 hours on low or 6–7 hours on high. Remove the bouquet garni. Blend the butter and flour together thoroughly and stir into the hot casserole a dab at a time to thicken. Serve with rice and garnish with chopped parsley.

serves 4–5

Beef bourguignon

2 tablespoons flour
1 kg (2¼ lb) stewing beef, chuck, blade
or shin, diced
90 g (3 oz) butter
1 tablespoon tomato paste
2 garlic cloves, crushed
750 ml (24 fl oz / 3 cups) burgundy
625 ml (21 fl oz / 2½ cups) beef stock

salt and pepper, to taste
1 bouquet garni
60 g (2 oz) pickled pork or bacon, diced
12 small onions
2 carrots, sliced
12 button (white) mushrooms
chopped parsley, to garnish

1. Preheat the oven to 160°C/325°F/Gas mark 3. Coat the diced beef with the flour. Melt the butter in a large pot, the fry the meat for 5 minutes. Add tomato paste and garlic and cook for another 5 minutes. Add burgundy and stock, season lightly with salt and pepper and add bouquet garni.
2. Cover and cook in the oven for 2½–3 hours, or until tender.
3. In a frying pan, fry the pickled pork or bacon lightly. Add the onions and carrots and cook over a moderate heat until evenly browned. Add pork or bacon and the mushrooms to the pot about 15 minutes before cooking is finished. Adjust the consistency and seasoning if necessary and serve hot, sprinkled with chopped parsley.

Note: The traditional recipe has 2 tablespoons of brandy added in the final stage along with the mushrooms.

serves 6

Beef stroganoff

90 g (3 oz) butter
1 large onion, thinly sliced
250 g (9 oz) mushrooms, peeled and sliced
750 g (1 lb 10 oz) fillet steak, trimmed of fat and cut into thin strips
1½ teaspoons salt
freshly ground black pepper, to taste
pinch of nutmeg
300 g (10½ oz) sour cream
parsley, chopped, to garnish

1. Melt 60 g (2 oz) of the butter in a heavy frying pan and sauté the onion until soft. Add the mushrooms and cook for 5 minutes. Place the mixture in a bowl and keep warm.

2. Melt the remaining butter in pan and quickly brown the beef strips on all sides. Do this stage in two lots unless you have a very large frying pan. Take the pan off the heat and add the onion, mushrooms, salt, pepper and nutmeg. Stir well to blend, then replace the pan over a medium heat and pour in the sour cream. Stir gently until heated through. Do not allow the sauce to boil.

3. Serve with boiled rice, cooked cabbage or coleslaw.

serves 4

Perfect t-bone steak

4 t-bone steaks
2 teaspoons crushed garlic
2 teaspoons oil
salt and pepper

FOR THE GARLIC BUTTER
55g (2 oz) butter
1 teaspoon crushed garlic
1 tablespoon parsley flakes
2 teaspoons lemon juice

1. Combine the garlic butter ingredients. Spoon into a small pot and set aside. Bring the steaks to room temperature. Mix the garlic, oil and salt and pepper together. Rub onto both sides of the steak. Let stand for 10–15 minutes at room temperature.
2. Heat the barbecue until hot and oil the grill (broiler) bars. Arrange the steaks and sear for 1 minute on each side. Move the steaks to the cooler part of the barbecue to continue cooking over moderate heat, or reduce the heat. If the heat cannot be reduced then elevate the steaks on a wire rack placed on the grill bars. Cook for 5–6 minutes for rare, 7–10 minutes for medium and 10–14 minutes for well done. Turn during cooking.
3. Serve on a heated steak plate and top with a dollop of garlic butter. Serve with potatoes.

Note: To tenderise tough meat, rub in a mixture of malt vinegar and cooking oil and allow to stand for about 2 hours.

serves 4

Braised lamb shanks

2 tablespoons olive oil
4 lamb shanks
1 onion, chopped
1 clove garlic (optional), crushed
1 carrot, diced
90 g (3 oz) celery, diced

225 g (8 oz) skinned, chopped tomatoes
or canned tomatoes
1 teaspoon salt
¼ teaspoon freshly ground black pepper
½ teaspoon sugar
60 ml (¼ cup) beef stock, or water
1 teaspoon Worcestershire sauce

1. Heat the oil in a frying pan and brown the lamb shanks over a moderately high heat. Pour off most of the oil and reduce the heat. Add the onion, garlic (if using), carrot and celery and cook until the onion is soft. Stir in the tomatoes, salt, pepper, sugar, stock and Worcestershire sauce. Spoon some of the vegetable mixture over the shanks. Place a lid on the pan and simmer for 2 hours, or until tender. Adjust the flavour before serving.
2. Serve with mashed potatoes and steamed vegetables.

serves 4

Irish stew

1 kg (2¼ lb) potatoes, peeled
salt and pepper, to taste
1 kg (2¼ lb) lamb neck chops, trimmed of fat
500 g (1 lb 2 oz) white onions, thickly sliced
bunch of herbs (parsley, thyme, rosemary)
1 bay leaf
625 ml (2½ cups) beef stock
1 tablespoon extra parsley, finely chopped, to garnish

1. Preheat the oven to 160°C (325°F/Gas mark 3). Cut 3–4 potatoes into thick slices and cut the remaining potatoes in half.
2. Place sliced potatoes in an ovenproof casserole dish and season with salt and pepper. Cover with meat, then add onions and halved potatoes, and season again. Add herbs, bay leaf and stock.
3. Cover the casserole dish and cook in the oven for 2–2½ hours or until the meat is tender. Remove the herbs and bay leaf from the casserole and sprinkle with chopped parsley before serving.

serves 5–6

Veal osso bucco

4 large veal shanks (osso bucco),
about 150 g (5 oz) each
30 g (1 oz) seasoned plain (all-purpose) flour
60 ml (2 fl oz / ¼ cup) olive oil
1 onion, finely chopped
1 garlic, clove crushed
6 fl oz (175 ml / ¾ cup) tomato pasta sauce

4 fl oz (125 ml / ½ cup) beef stock
400 g (14 oz) can diced tomatoes
2 carrots, sliced
2 stalks celery, sliced
finely grated zest of 1 lemon, plus strips to garnish
400 g (14 oz) can cannellini beans, drained
2 tablespoons (¼ cup) fresh parsley, chopped

1. Coat the veal shanks lightly in seasoned flour. Heat 2 tablespoons of oil in a large saucepan over medium–high heat. Brown the veal shanks, then remove and set aside.
2. Heat the remaining oil, add the onion and garlic and cook for 2–3 minutes, or until soft. Add the tomato pasta sauce, stock, tomatoes, carrots, celery and lemon zest. Return the veal to the pan.
3. Cover and simmer for 35–40 minutes, or until tender. Add a little more stock, if needed. Stir in the beans and parsley and cook until heated through. Garnish with extra lemon zest. Serve with mashed potatoes or polenta.

Note: If you have time, simmer the meat over low heat for as long as possible until the meat starts to fall off the bone.

serves 4

Boiled corned silverside with white sauce

1.5–2 kg (3–4½ lb) piece corned silverside
(or brisket), rinsed
1 tablespoon brown sugar
12 whole black peppercorns
1 bay leaf
1 tablespoon vinegar
boiled carrots and onions and parsley sprigs,
to garnish

For the white sauce
30 g (1 oz) butter
30 g (1 oz) plain (all-purpose) flour
315 ml (10 fl oz/1¼ cups) milk
salt
nutmeg or freshly ground black pepper, to taste

1. Place silverside in a deep saucepan and cover with cold water. Add the remaining ingredients. Bring to simmering point and cook, covered, for 2 hours.
2. Garnish with carrots and onions and sprigs of parsley, and serve with white sauce.
3. To make white sauce: melt the butter in a saucepan over a low heat, then remove from the heat and stir in the flour. Return to heat and cook gently for a few minutes, making sure that the roux does not brown. Remove the pan from the heat and gradually blend in the cold milk. Replace the pan on the heat and bring to the boil. Reduce the heat and cook, stirring with a wooden spoon, until smooth. Season well. If any lumps have formed, whisk briskly.

Note: Corned silverside can also be served cold. Allow to cool in the cooking liquid, and when cold, wrap in plastic clingwrap or aluminium foil and store in the refrigerator.

serves 6–8

Shepherd's pie

1 tablespoon olive oil
1 onion, finely chopped
2 tomatoes, skinned and chopped
340 g (12 oz) minced (ground) beeff
generous pinch of mixed herbs
salt and pepper, to taste
315 ml (1¼ cups) beef stock
500 g (1 lb 2 oz) mashed potato
30 g (1 oz) butter

1. Preheat the oven to 200°C (400°F/Gas mark 6). In a frying pan, heat the olive oil and fry the onion for 3 minutes. Add the tomatoes and meat and heat together for 2–3 minutes. Stir in the herbs, seasoning and stock, add less stock if you desire a thicker consistency.
2. Put the meat mixture into a pie dish and cover with mashed potato. Use a fork to score the edges, or create any other design you like. Dot tiny pieces of butter around on the potato to help it brown. Bake in the centre of the oven until the top is crisp and golden, about 25 minutes.

serves 4

Beef pie

2 tablespoons vegetable oil
1 kg (2 lb 2 oz) blade or topside steak, cubed
1 onion, chopped
2 tablespoons plain (all-purpose) flour
2 beef stock cubes, crumbled
1 teaspoon Vegemite or yeast extract
1 tablespoon tomato paste

½ teaspoon salt
2 tablespoons (¼ cup) parsley, chopped
1 teaspoon Worcestershire sauce
1 teaspoon Tabasco sauce
225 g/8 oz puff pastry
2 tablespoons milk

1. Heat the oil in frying pan and brown the beef and onion, then transfer to the meat and onions to a slow cooker using a slotted spoon. Add the flour to the juices in the pan, brown it, and pour in 250 ml (8 fl oz/1 cup) water. Add the stock cubes, Vegemite or yeast extract, tomato paste and salt and bring to the boil, stirring.
2. Pour the liquid into the slow cooker with the parsley, Worcestershire and Tabasco sauces, to taste, and cook on low for at least 6–8 hours or overnight. Test the meat for tenderness, then spoon the beef mixture into a greased pie dish and allow to cool.
3. Preheat the oven to 190°C/375°F/Gas mark 5. Slice the puff pastry into long strips. Brush the rim of the pie dish with a little milk and fit a pastry strip around the wet rim, then use the remaining strips to create a lattice across the meat. Brush lightly with milk and bake for 25–30 minutes.

serves 6

Steak and kidney pie

2 sheep's kidneys, skinned, halved and cored
1 teaspoon salt
freshly ground black pepper, to taste
2 tablespoons plain (all-purpose) flour
2 tablespoons butter
500 g (1 lb 2 oz) casserole steak (chuck, blade, flank, skirt or round), trimmed and
cut into 1 cm (½ in) cubes
125 ml (4 fl oz / ½ cup) water
340 g (12 oz) flaky pastry or puff pastry
2 tablespoons parsley, chopped
1 egg, beaten

1. Cut the kidney into small pieces. Season the flour with salt and pepper, then coat the meat and kidneys with the flour.
2. Melt the butter in a heavy pan (use one that has a lid) over a moderate heat and brown the steak and kidney, stirring continuously. Add water, cover tightly and simmer gently for 1 hour. Stir in parsley, then leave to cool.
3. Roll out the pastry to a circle that is 2.5 cm (1 in) larger than the top of your pie dish. Cut a strip 1 cm (½ in) wide off the edge and place it on the dampened rim of the dish. Brush it with cold water. Spoon the steak and kidney into the dish. Place the remaining pastry on top of mixture and press the edges of the pastry onto the pastry rim to seal. Trim off the excess pastry and decorate the edge by flaking and fluting with the back of a fork. Glaze the pie with egg and cut a cross on top about 2 cm (¾ in) deep.
4. Bake in the oven for 20 minutes, then reduce the heat to moderately slow 160°C/325°F/ Gas mark 3 and bake for another 20 minutes.

serves 4

Bacon and egg pie

2 sheets puff pastry
1 medium brown onion, finely chopped
115 g (4 oz) bacon, diced
2 tablespoons spicy chutney
6 medium eggs
salt and pepper
1 tablespoon milk

1. Preheat the oven to 200°C/400°F/Gas mark 6 and lightly grease a 20 cm (8 in) square ovenproof dish. Line the dish with 1 sheet of pastry.
2. Scatter onion and bacon evenly over the pastry, then dot the chutney on top. Break the eggs evenly over the top, pricking the yolks so they run slightly. Season with salt and pepper.
3. Carefully position the second sheet of pastry over the filling, trimming the edges, and secure the pastry by pressing down the edges firmly using a fork. Brush the pastry with milk.
4. Bake for 40 minutes, or until risen and golden. Serve hot or cold with grilled (broiled) vine-ripened cherry tomatoes and a leafy green salad.

Note If you prefer, you can use chopped baby spinach instead of bacon in this recipe.

serves 6

Fish pie

*500 g (1 lb 2 oz) potatoes, peeled and cut into
even-sized pieces
salt and freshly ground black pepper
75 g (2½ oz) butter
2 eggs*

*500 g (17½ oz) cod fillets
250 g (9 oz) smoked haddock fillets
375 ml (12 fl oz / 1½ cups) whole milk
⅓ cup all-purpose (plain) flour
3 tablespoons (⅓ cup) fresh parsley, chopped*

1. Put the potatoes into a saucepan, cover with cold water, add ½ teaspoon of salt, then boil for 20 minutes, or until tender. Drain and return to the pan. Mash well with a potato masher or fork, then mix in two-thirds of the butter.
2. Meanwhile, boil the eggs for 10 minutes in a small pan. Cool under cold running water, then shell and roughly chop. Preheat the oven to 200°C/400°F/Gas mark 6.
3. Place the cod and haddock fillets skin-side down in a frying pan that is large enough to hold them in a single layer. Cover with milk and poach over a medium heat for 10 minutes, or until the fish turns opaque.
4. Drain the fish, reserving the milk for the sauce, then remove and discard any skin. Using a fork, flake the flesh into thick chunks, removing any bones.
5. Place the remaining butter in a large heavy pan. Melt over a low heat, add the flour and stir to form a smooth paste. Cook for 2 minutes, stirring, to remove the raw taste of the flour. Remove from the heat and add the milk little by little, stirring constantly so there are no lumps.
6. Return the pan to the heat and cook the sauce for 5–7 minutes, until quite thick. Remove from the heat again and gently stir in the fish, eggs and parsley. Season well, then pour into a 23 x 15 cm (9 x 6 in) ovenproof dish. Smooth the mashed potato on top, then fluff it up with a fork. Bake for 30 minutes, or until the top turns golden.

serves 4

Pasta bake

1 large onion, chopped
1 clove garlic, crushed
150 g (5 oz) lean bacon, chopped
3 large mushrooms, chopped
1 teaspoon paprika
1 teaspoon dried oregano leaves
1 tablespoon olive oil
500 g (1 lb 2 oz) lean minced (ground) beef
300 g (10½ oz) tomato salsa
½ red capsicum (bell pepper), chopped

1 oz (1 cup) basil leaves, chopped
2 bay leaves
500 g (1 lb 2 oz) spaghetti, cooked and drained
500 g (1 lb 2 oz) Cheddar cheese, grated (shredded)

FOR THE TOPPING
75 g (2½ oz) Cheddar cheese, grated (shredded)
2 eggs, beaten
60 g (2 oz / 1 cup) fresh breadcrumbs, toasted

1. Fry the onion, garlic, bacon, mushrooms, paprika and oregano in the olive oil until softened.
2. Add the beef mince and cook over a high heat until it changes colour and breaks into small pieces.
3. Add the salsa, capsicum, basil and bay leaves. Simmer for 30 minutes.
4. Preheat the oven to 180°C/350°F/Gas mark 4. Layer the spaghetti with the meat sauce and cheese into a large, shallow baking dish.
5. To make the topping, combine the cheese with the eggs. Pour over the top of the spaghetti bake, then sprinkle with the breadcrumbs.
6. Bake for 30 minutes until golden brown. Serve with a crisp green salad.

serves 6

Lasagne

2 tablespoons olive oil, plus extra for greasing
225 g (8 oz) minced (ground) beef
225 g (8 oz) minced (ground) pork
1 onion, finely chopped
1 garlic clove, finely chopped
1 teaspoon parsley, chopped
1 tube tomato paste

470 ml (16 oz) water
½ teaspoon salt
½ teaspoon freshly ground black pepper
225 g (8 oz) lasagne sheets
30 g (1 oz) mozzarella cheese, sliced thinly
250 g (8 oz) ricotta cheese, crumbed
2 tablespoons romano cheese, grated (shredded)

1. Heat the oil in a saucepan, add the beef and pork and brown with the onion, garlic and parsley. Stir in the tomato paste, water, salt and pepper and simmer for 1½ hours.
2. Preheat the oven to 180°C/350°F/Gas mark 4. Bring a large saucepan of water to the boil, add 1½ teaspoons salt and the lasagne sheets. Boil for 20 minutes, stirring constantly to prevent the noodles sticking, until tender. Drain.
3. In a greased casserole dish about 5 cm (2 in) deep, arrange alternate layers of lasagne sheets, sauce, mozzarella and ricotta cheese. Repeat the layers until the noodles and sauce and two cheeses are all used, ending with ricotta cheese. Sprinkle with grated romano cheese and bake for 25–30 minutes.

serves 4–6

Tortellini boscaiola

500 g (1 lb 2 oz) tortellini
1 tablespoon butter
3 shallots, chopped
175 g (6 oz) ham, thinly sliced
175 g (6 oz) mushrooms, sliced
125 ml (4 fl oz / ½ cup) chicken stock
375 ml (12 fl oz / 1½ cups) double (heavy) cream
freshly ground black pepper
40 g (1½ oz) Parmesan, grated (shredded)

1. Bring a large saucepan of salted water to the boil, add the pasta and cook for 8 minutes, or until just firm in the centre (*al dente*). Drain, set aside and keep warm.
2. Melt the butter in a frying pan over medium heat. Add the onions, ham and mushrooms and cook, stirring, for 4 minutes, or until the mushrooms are soft.
3. Stir in the stock, cream and black pepper and simmer for 6–8 minutes, or until the sauce reduces and thickens slightly.
4. To serve, spoon sauce over hot pasta, toss to combine and top with Parmesan.

serves 4

Spaghetti Bolognese

1 tablespoon olive oil
250 g (9 oz) minced (ground) beef
1 garlic clove, crushed
1 large onion (or 2 small onions),
finely grated (shredded)
500 g (1 lb 2 oz) peeled tomatoes, chopped
1 teaspoon oregano or basil

1 teaspoon salt
freshly ground black pepper, to taste
1 teaspoon sugar
3 tablespoons tomato paste
250 ml (8 fl oz / 1 cup) beef stock
250 g (9 oz) spaghetti
Parmesan, to garnish

1. Heat the oil in a frying pan, add the meat, garlic and onion and brown lightly. Add the tomatoes, oregano, salt, pepper and sugar.
2. In a small bowl, blend the tomato paste with the stock. Add this to the mixture in the frying pan. Simmer for 30 minutes, uncovered, so that sauce thickens slightly.
3. When the sauce is almost ready, cook the spaghetti in boiling salted water until tender (about 20 minutes). Drain the spaghetti, and place on a hot serving dish or plate. Pour hot sauce over the spaghetti and sprinkle with Parmesan. Serve additional cheese in a small bowl.

serves 4

Spaghetti carbonara

250–375 g (8–12 oz) fettucine
2 tablespoons olive oil
3 rashers (strips) bacon, finely diced
2 eggs
45 g (1½ oz) Parmesan, grated (shredded)
250 ml (8 fl oz / 1 cup) single (light) cream
freshly ground black pepper, to taste

1. Add the fettucine into boiling, salted water and cook for 8 minutes or until *al dente*.
2. Just before the fettucine is ready, heat the oil and fry the bacon.
3. In a bowl, beat in the eggs and add the cheese.
4. Drain the pasta and return it to the hot saucepan. Add the cheese mixture, cream, plenty of black pepper and the crisp bacon. Mix well. Place the saucepan over a low heat for 1 minute or so, stirring constantly.
5. Transfer to a hot dish and serve immediately.

serves 4

Spaghetti with meatballs

250 g (8 oz) spaghetti or thin spaghetti
Parmesan, shaved, to garnish

FOR THE TOMATO SAUCE
400 g (14 oz) can whole tomatoes
250 ml (8 fl oz / 1 cup) Italian tomato sauce (see
following page)
115 g (4 oz) tomato paste
60 ml (2 fl oz / ¼ cup) water
60 ml (2 fl oz / ¼ cup) red wine (or water)
2 bay leaves, crushed
2 tablespoons parsley, chopped
1 garlic clove, crushed

FOR THE MEATBALLS
4 slices white bread
450 g (1 lb) minced (ground) chuck or round steak
1 tablespoon parmesan cheese, grated
1 tablespoon parsley, chopped
1 tablespoon onion, grated
2 teaspoons salt
¼ teaspoon black pepper
¼ teaspoon oregano
1 egg
3 tablespoons olive oil

1. To make tomato sauce, combine all the ingredients in a large pan. Simmer until thick, stirring occasionally for about 10 minutes.
2. To make meatballs, put the bread in a small bowl, add enough water to cover, and let stand for 2 minutes. Remove the bread and squeeze out the excess water. In a larger bowl, combine the bread with the meat, Parmesan, parsley, onion, salt, pepper, oregano and egg. Mix lightly until thoroughly combined. Shape into small balls. Heat the oil in a frying pan and brown the meatballs on all sides.
3. Add the meatballs to the sauce and simmer for 15–20 minutes. Meanwhile, cook the spaghetti in salted, boiling water according to the packet instructions. Drain the spaghetti and place on a hot serving dish or plate. Top with meatballs and sauce and serve with Parmesan.

serves 4–6

Italian tomato sauce

2 tablespoons olive oil

1 small onion, finely chopped

2 garlic cloves, crushed

1 kg (2¼ lb) tomatoes, skinned, seeded and chopped or 2 x 400 g

(14 oz) cans whole tomatoes, diced

½ teaspoon salt

½ teaspoon caster (superfine) sugar, or to taste

¼ teaspoon freshly ground black pepper

2 leaves basil

1 sprig oregano

1 bay leaf

1 tablespoon tomato paste

1. In a large saucepan, heat the oil. Add the onion and garlic and cook for 5–6 minutes, stirring until the onion is translucent. Add the tomatoes and all the other ingredients. Return to the heat and bring to the boil. Reduce the heat, cover, and simmer for 45 minutes, stirring occasionally.

2. Purée the sauce in a blender or food processor if you would like a smooth consistency.

serves 4

Mushroom and onion risotto

30 g (1 oz) butter
1 small onion, chopped or sliced
1 rasher (strip) bacon, diced
12 button (white) mushrooms, sliced
280 g (10 oz) arborio rice
13 fl oz (375 ml) chicken stock, boiling
115 g (4 oz) cheese, grated (shredded)
salt and freshly ground black pepper, to taste

1. Melt the butter in a heavy pan, and fry the onion, bacon and mushrooms, stirring once or twice, for 3–4 minutes. Stir in the rice and cook for 1–2 minutes.
2. Pour in the hot stock gradually, stirring constantly until the liquid is absorbed. Continue stirring while adding stock until all the liquid is absorbed each time. Cook the rice for 30 minutes, or until it is tender. Add extra hot water or stock, if necessary.
3. Stir through the cheese, and season with salt and pepper. Serve immediately with fresh herbs, accompanied with green salad.

serves 4

Bacon and pea risotto

3 rashers (strips) rindless bacon, cut into thin strips
1 onion, finely chopped
300 g (10½ oz / 1½ cups) arborio rice
1 teaspoon dried sage
1.25 l (2¼ pints / 5 cups) chicken stock, heated
225 g (8 oz / 2 cups) frozen peas
freshly ground black pepper
1½ oz (45g) Parmesan cheese

1. In a large saucepan, sauté the bacon and onion for about 5 minutes, or until the onion is soft.
2. Add the rice and sage and stir to coat the rice with the bacon and onion mixture.
3. Pour 1 ladle of hot stock into the rice mixture and cook, stirring constantly, until the liquid is absorbed. Repeat with another ladle of stock.
4. Continue adding stock 1 ladle at a time until the rice is tender and all the liquid has been absorbed. With the last addition of stock, add the peas.
5. When all the stock is absorbed, season the risotto with pepper and ladle into bowls. Top with Parmesan and serve immediately.

serves 4

Fried rice

228 g (8 oz) rice, uncooked
250 g (9 oz) lean pork, chopped
oil, for frying
2 eggs
250 g (9 oz) shrimp (prawns), cooked and chopped
5 mushrooms, thinly sliced

4 shallots, chopped
salt, to taste
4 teaspoons soy sauce

1. Wash the rice several times in cold water to remove the excess starch. Tip into a saucepan of boiling, salted water and cook for 15 minutes, or until the grains are just tender—do not overcook. Drain the rice and allow to cool completely.
2. In a frying pan, heat 1 teaspoon of the oil and fry the pork until lightly browned.
3. Beat the eggs lightly in a bowl, then heat 1 teaspoon of oil in a frying pan and fry as a thin pancake or omelette. Remove from the pan and slice into strips.
4. Pour enough oil into a large pan to cover the base and heat it. When hot, add the rice slowly, to avoid clumping, and stir for about 10 minutes, or until the rice is thoroughly heated through. Stir vigorously, breaking up any lumps.
5. Add the cooked pork, shrimp, mushrooms, shallots and salt, then fold in the egg pieces (or beaten egg) and soy sauce. Mix well and serve.

serves 4–6

Quiche

FOR THE PASTRY

250 g (9 oz) self-raising (self-rising) flour
175 g (6 oz) hard butter, grated (shredded)
1 egg yolk
60 ml (2 fl oz / ¼ cup) cold milk

FOR THE FILLING

625 ml (22 fl oz / 2½ cups) milk
3 eggs
3 spring onions (scallions), chopped
115 g (4 oz) ham, chopped
115 g (4 oz) cheese, grated (shredded)

1. Preheat the oven to 200°C (400°F/Gas mark 6).
2. To make the pastry, sift the flour into a large bowl and add the butter. Rub the fat into the flour with your fingertips until the mixture resembles fine breadcrumbs. Make a hollow in the centre and drop in the egg yolk. Mix to combine using a spoon or the blunt blade of a knife. Pour in the milk, a little at a time, and combine as you go, until you can make a ball of pastry that sticks together. On a floured surface, roll out the pastry until it is 5 mm (¼ in) thick. Place the pastry in a flan ring or pie dish and trim off the edges. Cover and refrigerate, for about 30 minutes.
3. To make the filling, pour milk into a large bowl, break eggs in and beat with an egg beater. Stir onion and ham into the mixture and pour into the pastry shell. Scatter cheese over the top, then bake or 45 minutes, or until the quiche is set.

serves 4

Bouillabaisse

*3 kg (6 lb 10 oz) mixed fish and seafood, including
firm white fish fillets, shrimp (prawns), mussels, crab
and calamari rings*
60 ml (2 fl oz / ¼ cup) olive oil
2 garlic cloves, crushed
2 large onions, chopped
2 leeks, sliced
2 x 400 g (14 oz) cans tomatoes
165 ml (5½ fl oz / ⅔ cup) fish stock

1 teaspoon dried thyme
2 tablespoons fresh basil, chopped
2 tablespoons fresh parsley, chopped
2 bay leaves
2 tablespoons orange zest, finely grated (shredded)
1 teaspoon saffron threads
165 ml (5½ fl oz / ⅔ cup) dry white wine
freshly ground black pepper

1. Remove any bones and skin from the fish fillets and cut into 2 cm (¾ in) cubes. Peel and devein the shrimp, leaving the tails intact. Scrub and remove the beards from the mussels. Cut the crab into quarters. Set aside.
2. Heat a slow cooker on a high setting, then add the oil, garlic, onions, leeks, tomatoes and stock and cook for 1½ hours. Add the thyme, basil, parsley, bay leaves, orange rind, saffron and wine. Cook for 30 minutes.
3. Add the fish and crab and cook for 1 hour. Add the remaining seafood and cook for 1 hour longer, or until all the fish and seafood are cooked. Season to taste with black pepper.

serves 6

SIDE DISHES

Side dishes

The side dishes presented here are all familiar favourites; everyday dishes that we love and enjoy. And though these dishes are not the main event in culinary terms, they help make a meal memorable. Often an interesting side dish can be served alongside a plain cut of grilled (broiled) or roasted meat, adding interest, nutritional value and colour to the dinner plate.

Who doesn't love a side helping of creamy mashed potato, or indulgent potato gratin? Jacket potatoes are often a staple dish that can be the main ingredient rather than a side, especially when topped with a range of delicious and tasty fillings. Alongside that recipe you'll find plenty of potato and salad dishes as well as vegetable accompaniments that make a meal complete. From sweet and creamy corn kernels to flavourful roasted vegetables, this collection of dishes will see you through any everyday meal or dinner party situation. Pair a potato dish with a vegetable dish and serve with a main course, allowing enough vegetables for each person to half-fill the plate. And since they're the least expensive part of any meal, and packed with nutritional value it makes sense to serve plenty.

Baked potatoes

4 medium potatoes
1 head of garlic
2 rosemary sprigs

1. Preheat the oven to 200°C/400°F/Gas mark 6.
2. Scrub the potatoes under running water.
3. Score with a knife or prick all over with a skewer or a fork to stop them exploding in the oven.
4. Add the head of garlic and the rosemary.
5. Put potatoes at the back of the centre shelf in the oven and bake for 1½ hours.

Note: Do not turn the oven down at all while the potatoes are cooking—
they will go soft immediately.

serves 4

Potato gratin

900 g (2 lbs) potatoes, thinly sliced
2 large onions, thinly sliced
2 tablespoons fresh chives, chopped
freshly ground black pepper
300 ml (10 fl oz / 1¼ cups) natural (plain) yogurt
250 ml (8 fl oz / 1 cup) double (heavy) cream
50 g (1¾ oz) Parmesan, shaved

1. Layer the potatoes, onions, chives and pepper to taste in six lightly greased individual ovenproof dishes.
2. Place the yogurt and cream in a bowl and mix to combine. Carefully pour the yogurt mixture over the potatoes and scatter with the cheese. Bake for 45 minutes, or until the potatoes are tender and the top is golden.

serves 6

Mashed potato

4 medium potatoes, peeled, cut into large chunks
125 ml (4 fl oz / ½ cup) milk
30 g (1 oz) butter
60 g (2 oz) cheese, grated (shredded)
salt and freshly ground black pepper, to taste

1. Put the potatoes into a saucepan, cover with cold, and season lightly with salt. Bring to the boil and cook gently, covered, for 20–30 minutes, until the potatoes are easily pierced with a fork. Drain thoroughly, then shake the pan over heat for 1 or 2 minutes until all surplus moisture has evaporated and the potatoes are dry.
2. Mash the potatoes, then beat with a wooden spoon until very smooth. In a saucepan, heat the milk and butter. Once the liquid is hot, add to the potatoes and beat until light and fluffy. Add the cheese and stir through until melted. Season with salt and pepper. Serve immediately.

serves 4

French fries

6 large potatoes
300 ml (10½ fl oz) vegetable oil, for deep-frying
salt, to taste

1. Peel the potatoes and cut into chips 5 x 1 x 1 cm (2 x ½ x ½ in). Place in a large bowl and cover with ice cold water for at least 30 minutes. Dry thoroughly in a clean dish towel.
2. Heat the oil until very hot—a 2.5 cm (1 in) cube of bread will brown in 1 minute when the oil is hot enough. Put the fries in a frying basket and lower into the oil. The fries should be completely covered. Fry until tender but not brown, about 10 minutes. Remove the fries from the oil and drain. Set aside until just before serving.
3. Reheat the oil and cook the fries until golden, crisp and slightly puffy. Drain very well, sprinkle with salt, and serve immediately.

Variation: For potato straws, cut potatoes into matchsticks, then prepare and fry as above.

serves 2

Cucumber salad

3 cucumbers, washed, dried and thinly sliced
1 tablespoon salt
2 garlic cloves, cut into slivers
175 ml (6 fl oz / ¾ cup) balsamic vinegar
2 tablespoons sugar
freshly ground white pepper
1 tablespoon parsley or fresh dill, chopped, to garnish

1. Arrange the cucumber slices in a deep bowl and sprinkle with salt. Cover with a small plate that fits inside the bowl and place a heavy weight on top. Set aside at room temperature for 2 hours.
2. Place the garlic slivers in the vinegar and set aside for at least 30 minutes.
3. Drain the juice from the cucumber; squeeze the cucumber as dry as possible. Add sugar and pepper to the garlic-flavoured vinegar and pour over the cucumber. Taste and adjust the seasoning, if necessary. Cover tightly and chill thoroughly.
4. Before serving, drain the vinegar from the cucumber and sprinkle the dish with chopped parsley or dill.

serves 6–8

Coleslaw

½ small cabbage, shredded
2 carrots, grated
1 onion, grated
1 garlic clove, crushed (optional)
⅔ stalk celery, sliced
2 tablespoons olive oil
125 ml (4 fl oz / ½ cup) mayonnaise
1 teaspoon salt
freshly ground black pepper, to taste
pinch of caster (superfine) sugar

1. Mix the cabbage, carrots, onion, garlic and celery in a large salad bowl.
2. Combine the olive oil, mayonnaise, salt, pepper and sugar in a separate bowl. Stir the dressing through the salad and serve immediately.

serves 4–6

Mixed salad

1 red bell pepper (capsicum), seeded and
cut into quarters
3 vine-ripened tomatoes, cut into wedges
1 tablespoon olive oil
1 small cucumber, sliced
1 small red onion, finely chopped
85 g (3 oz / ½ cup) black olives
150 g (5 oz) mixed greens such as curly endive,
baby spinach, butter lettuce, and watercress

2 tablespoons or ¼ cup fresh coriander (cilantro)

FOR THE DRESSING
60 ml (2 fl oz / ¼ cup) extra-virgin olive oil
1 tablespoon lemon juice
1 tablespoon red wine vinegar
½ teaspoon sugar
salt and freshly ground black pepper

1. Place the bell pepper on a baking sheet and grill (broil) for 6–8 minutes, or until the skin is blistered and blackened. Leave to cool. Remove the skin and thinly slice.
2. Preheat the oven to 180°C/350°F/Gas mark 4. Place the tomatoes on a baking sheet lined with baking paper. Lightly spray or brush with olive oil and season with salt and pepper. Bake for 15–20 minutes, or until just soft. Set aside.
3. Combine the roasted bell pepper, baked tomatoes, cucumber, red onion, olives, salad leaves, and chopped coriander in a large serving bowl.
4. Combine the dressing ingredients in a small bowl. Pour the dressing over the salad and toss to combine.

serves 4

Greek salad

2 English cucumbers, sliced
4 Roma tomatoes, quartered
2 red onions, quartered
3 oz (85 g) feta, crumbled
85 g (3 oz / ½ cup) Kalamata olives, left whole
3 tablespoons extra-virgin olive oil
2 tablespoons red wine vinegar
pinch of sea salt
freshly ground black pepper
2 tablespoons or ¼ cup oregano leaves

1. Place the cucumber, tomatoes, onion, feta, and olives in a bowl.
2. Whisk together the olive oil and vinegar in a separate bowl. Pour the dressing over the salad, then season with salt and pepper.
3. Garnish with oregano leaves. Serve the salad on its own or with fresh bread.

serves 4

Corn on the cob

1. Strip the silk off the corn. Brush the corn with melted butter and sprinkle with salt and freshly ground black pepper. Replace the husks and secure in three places with string.
2. Barbecue the corn cobs over hot coals for 15–20 minutes, or until tender, turning frequently. When cooked, the husks will be dry and brown and the corn will be golden brown. Serve with melted butter and salt and pepper.

Variation: After stripping off the silk, wrap a rindless bacon rasher (strip) around each corn cob and secure at the ends with cocktail sticks. Replace the husks and proceed as above.

Select young, tender corn cobs by checking they are bright yellow in colour and not wrinkled.

You can remove husks from corn cobs completely. If you do this, brush the corn with melted butter and season with salt and pepper, then wrap each corn cob in aluminium foil and barbecue over hot coals for 20 minutes, or until tender. Serve as above.

serves 4

Roasted vegetables

3 red onions, quartered
3 potatoes, scrubbed and cut into wedges
2 zucchini (courgettes), thickly sliced
2 yellow bell peppers (capsicums), seeded and thickly sliced
4 tomatoes, halved
2 tablespoons olive oil
sea salt and freshly ground black pepper
Parmesan shavings

FOR THE DRESSING
3 tablespoons extra virgin olive oil
2 tablespoons honey
1 tablespoon balsamic vinegar
juice and finely grated zest of ½ lemon

1. Preheat the oven to 200°C/400°F/Gas mark 6. Place all the vegetables in a shallow roasting tin (pan), drizzle with olive oil and season. Shake the tin gently to ensure the vegetables are well coated with the oil and seasoning. Bake for about 35 minutes, until the vegetables are very tender and slightly charred at the edges.
2. Meanwhile, mix all the dressing ingredients together. When the vegetables are cooked, add the dressing and toss well. Divide between four plates, then top with Parmesan shavings.

serves 4

Minted peas

450 g (1 lb/4 cups) fresh or frozen peas
5 whole sprigs mint, and 5 sprigs with stalks removed and leaves shredded
45 g (1½ oz) butter
salt and white pepper

1. Put the peas in a saucepan and pour in enough water to just cover. Add the whole mint sprigs. Bring to the boil and simmer for 5 minutes if fresh, 2 minutes if frozen.
2. Meanwhile, in another small saucepan set over a low heat, melt the butter and add the shredded mint to infuse.
3. When the peas are cooked, drain and discard the mint. Return the peas to the saucepan, add the melted butter and shredded mint, and stir over a low heat until combined. Season with salt and white pepper.

serves 6

Cauliflower cheese

450 g (1 lb) cauliflower, cut into small florets
15 g (½ oz / ¼ cup) fresh breadcrumbs
2 tablespoons or ¼ small bunch flat-leaf parsley

FOR THE CHEESE SAUCE
30 g (1 oz) butter, plus extra for greasing
30 g (1 oz / ¼ cup) plain (all-purpose) flour

280 ml (10 fl oz / 1¼ cups) milk, warmed
1 teaspoon wholegrain mustard
75 g (2½ oz) Parmesan, shaved, at room temperature
salt and white pepper

1. Lightly butter a heatproof dish. Cook the cauliflower in a saucepan of lightly salted boiling water for 8 minutes, or until just tender. Drain thoroughly, then transfer to the prepared dish and keep warm.
2. To make the cheese sauce, melt the butter in a pan over low heat. Stir in the flour and cook for 1 minute, or until lightly coloured and bubbling. Remove from the heat and gradually stir in the milk and mustard. If lumps form, press the mixture through a strainer. Return to the heat and stir constantly until the sauce simmers and thickens. Reduce the heat and simmer for another 2 minutes, then remove from the heat again.
3. Add the Parmesan and stir until thoroughly combined. Season with salt and white pepper and pour over the cauliflower.
4. Combine the breadcrumbs and parsley and sprinkle evenly on top of the sauce. Grill (broil) under a medium heat until the top is golden brown. Serve immediately.

serves 4

DESSERTS

Desserts

With a co-operative oven and a touch of skill, anyone can whip up a creation that will dazzle guests, silence a mother-in-law and satisfy a grumbling belly. Whether it's a homemade loaf cake, a decadent pudding or a plate of cookies, the recipes in this chapter are classic crowd-pleasers. And who doesn't love a dessert? Maybe you even plan your main course based upon what's on offer for the dessert course, always making sure to leave a little space for a sweet treat at the end of the meal?

Cakes and desserts are not just a finale for a meal, many of these recipes are perfect for serving at any time, whether it's a sweet treat for yourself, morning coffee with friends or afternoon tea with neighbours. Cakes and cookies are easy to make as long as you adhere rigidly to the recipe requirements and you are using good quality bakeware that won't bend and buckle with the heat of the oven. Use these recipes to make cakes for the school fête or fundraising get-togethers. Everyone loves shortbread and carrot cake. What's not to love?

This chapter contains recipes that are both contemporary and traditional. Rice pudding is inexpensive to make and will feed a large family as an everyday pud. Everyone has different ideas of how it should taste and look - a thick skin topping, or no skin, a sprinkling of nutmeg, or filled with rum-soaked dried fruit. Baked apples have stood the test of time too. This is a great dessert when these fruits are plentiful in the autumn and winter months. Serve with a helping of custard or cream, if you like. Add to your repertoire classic egg custard and lemon meringue pie, comforting bread and butter pudding - perfect if there's likely to be leftovers to nibble on from the refrigerator, and who can resist light and airy crème caramel, stodgy chocolate brownies or imperious sacher torte?

Note Some pastry recipes call for 'blind baking'. This is a process of pre-baking the pastry case before it is filled. It's a necessary step when the filling isn't going to be baked, or when the filling takes less time to bake than the pastry. Blind baking lends other useful effects, such as preventing the crust from becoming soggy later, and helps to form a nice, firm case for the filling. Instructions for blind baking are generally given in the relevant recipes. Recipes may advise the use of baking beans and a lining of baking paper, which is discarded when the pastry case is part baked.

Plum pudding

2 tablespoons plum jelly (jam)
60 g (2 oz) butter, plus extra for greasing
60 g (2 oz / ¼ cup) sugar
1 egg
60 g (2 oz / ½ cup) plain (all-purpose) flour
1 teaspoon baking powder
1 tablespoon milk

1. Set a pan that is large enough to fit a 13 x 6 cm (5 x 2 in) deep fluted pudding basin on the stovetop. Fill with enough water to come halfway up the pudding basin. Make sure that you have a tight-fitting lid for the saucepan.
2. Grease the pudding basin. Cut a piece of greaseproof (baking) paper large enough to fit the top of the basin. The paper should be larger than the basin so that it will not let any water in when the pudding is steaming.
3. Put the plum jelly in the base of the pudding basin.
4. In a mixing bowl, cream the butter, sugar and egg together with a wooden spoon until light and fluffy. Fold in the sifted flour and baking powder. Stir in the milk and pour the batter into the pudding basin. Lower the pudding into the boiling water. Loosely place the greaseproof paper on top.
5. Fit the lid on the saucepan and keep the water boiling for about 40 minutes. Keep checking to make sure the pan has not boiled dry. When cooked, turn the pudding out onto a plate and serve with custard or ice cream.

serves 3

Baked apples

8 prunes, pitted and chopped
2 tablespoons raisins
4 cooking apples, cored
4 tablespoons honey
30 g (1 oz) butter
4 tablespoons water
vanilla custard sauce, to serve

1. Preheat the oven to 180°C/350°F/Gas mark 4. In a bowl, combine the prunes with the raisins. Place the apples in a baking dish and stuff the empty cores with the prunes and raisins. Pour honey over the apples and dot with butter. Add a little water to the baking dish.
2. Bake for ¾–1 hour, or until the apples are tender. Serve hot with vanilla custard sauce.

serves 8

Creamy rice pudding

1. Reserve a little orange zest to decorate, then mix the rice, in a bowl, with all the other ingredients. Lightly grease the slow cooker interior and spoon in the pudding mixture.
2. Cook on high for approximately 1–2 hours or on low for 4–6 hours. Stir occasionally during the first hour of cooking. Serve with a little cream and a pinch of grated orange zest.

serves 6

Bread and butter pudding

2 large or 4 small slices of bread
butter, for spreading
60 g (2 oz) dried fruit
2 eggs
1 tablespoon caster (superfine) sugar, plus extra for sprinkling
150 ml (5 fl oz /⅔ cup) milk
pinch of nutmeg, grated

1. Preheat oven to 180°C/350°F/Gas mark 4. Generously butter the bread slices. Trim off the crusts. Cut the bread into small pieces and arrange in a shallow baking dish. Sprinkle over the dried fruit
2. To make custard, whisk the eggs in a bowl with a fork. Beat in the sugar and warm milk. Pour over the bread and make sure all of the bread is immersed in the eggy mixture. Allow to stand for 30 minutes. Sprinkle nutmeg and sugar on top.
3. Bake for 5 minutes to 1 hour. Serve hot or cold.

serves 4

Lemon meringue tart

FOR THE PASTRY CASE

150 g (5 oz) butter, plus extra for greasing

75 g (2½ oz/⅓ cup) caster (superfine) sugar

½ teaspoon vanilla extract

1 small egg

225 g (8 oz/2 cups) plain (all-purpose) flour

½ teaspoon baking powder

pinch of salt

FOR THE FILLING AND TOPPING

4 tablespoons cornflour (corn starch)

160 g (5½ oz/¾ cup) sugar

juice of ½ lemon

2 egg yolks

2 tablespoons butter, softened

grated zest of 1 lemon

3 egg whites

75 g (2½ oz/⅓ cup) sugar

1. Preheat the oven to 200°C/400°F/Gas mark 6. To make the pastry, in a mixing bowl,, cream the butter and sugar with the vanilla until light and fluffy. Add the egg. Sift over the flour and baking powder in batches and mix into the creamed butter mixture.

2. Knead lightly until smooth, cover and refrigerate for at least 30 minutes. Grease and line a 23 cm (9 in) pie plate with the pastry, decorate the edge and prick the base with a fork. Line the pastry with baking paper and half-fill with baking beans and bake for 25 minutes. Dsicard the paper and beans and set the case aside to cool. Reduce the oven temperature to 180°C/350°F/Gas mark 4.

3. To make the lemon filling, in a pan, blend the cornflour and 160 g sugar with 250 ml (8 fl oz/1 cup) of water, the lemon juice and egg yolks. Stir over low heat until the mixture boils and thickens. Beat in the butter and lemon zest. Allow to cool and pour into the pastry case.

4. To make the meringue, beat the egg whites in a grease-free bowl until stiff. Gradually add the remaining sugar and continue beating until thick and glossy. Swirl over the top of the lemon filling and bake until the meringue is firm and lightly browned, about 25 minutes.

serves 6–8

Traditional custard tart

150 g (5 oz) shortcrust pastry
3 large eggs
1¾ oz (50 g / ¼ cup) sugar
10 fl oz (½ pint / 1¼ cups) milk
2 teaspoons freshly ground nutmeg

1. Preheat the oven to 200°C.400°F/Gas mark 6. Roll out the pastry and use it to line a shallow 18 cm (7 in) diameter springform cake tin (pan). Prick the pastry all over with a fork, line with baking paper and fill with baking beans, then bake blind for 10–15 minutes.
2. In a bowl, beat the eggs lightly with the sugar. In a separate pan, heat the milk until it begins to steam, then add the beaten egg and sugar mixture to it in a steady stream, while whisking continually to stop the eggs from scrambling.
3. Increase the heat to 220°C/430°F/Gas mark 8. Pour the mixture into the pastry case, sprinkle the top with ground nutmeg and bake in the centre of the oven for 10 minutes. Reduce the heat to 180°C/350°F/Gas mark 4 and bake for another 20–25 minutes until the custard is just set. Remember, it will become firmer as it cools down.

serves 6

Homeland jam tarts

1 sheet shortcrust pastry
210 g (7½ oz / 1½ cups) frozen raspberries
100 g (3½ oz / ½ cup) caster (superfine) sugar
juice of ½ lemon
icing (confectioners') sugar, to dust
Whipped cream, to serve

1. Preheat the oven to 200°C/400°F/Gas mark 6. Lightly grease an 18 cm (7 in) flan case.
2. Use the pastry and use to line the base and sides to form a tart case. Trim the excess pastry. Line with baking paper and fill with baking beans. Bake blind for 10–15 minutes, or until the pastry is light golden. Remove the baking paper and beans.
3. Put the raspberries and sugar in a pan, add the lemon juice and set over high heat, stirring constantly until thickened and jelly-like.
4. Remove the the pastry case from the flan tin. Spoon the jelly into the pastry case and allow to cool before serving. Dust with icing sugar and serve with whipped cream.

serves 6

Grand Marnier crème caramel

6 tablespoons white sugar
butter, for greasing
3 eggs
625 ml (20 fl oz / 2½ cups) milk
2 tablespoons Grand Marnier

1. Melt half the sugar slowly in a heavy pan. Do not stir, just allow to melt into toffee.
2. Grease 4 small heatproof crème caramel moulds, then pour the melted sugar quickly into the bases of the dishes, dividing it equally, and swirl around the sides as high as possible.
3. In a bowl, beat the eggs well and whisk into the milk with the Grand Marnier and the remaining sugar. Keep whisking until the sugar has dissolved, then pour the mixture into the caramel moulds and cover with foil. Place the moulds into slow cooker and pour sufficient cold water around the bases to come halfway up the sides. Cook on low for approximately 3–4 hours.
4. Remove the crème caramels from the slow cooker and chill thoroughly. Serve either in the moulds or very carefully turned out onto plates, with any caramel left behind spooned over the top.

serves 4

Cheesecake

<table>
<tr><td>

1 x 200 g (7 oz) plain sweet biscuits (cookies)
125 g (4½ oz) butter

</td><td>

225 g (8 oz) cream cheese
75 ml (2½ fl oz /⅓ cup) lemon juice
400 g (14 oz) can condensed milk
whipped cream, to decorate
lemon zest, thinly sliced, to decorate

</td></tr>
</table>

1. To make the crust, put biscuits in a plastic bag and seal the top with an elastic band or twist tie. Using a rolling pin, crush the biscuits in the bag—you will need to roll again and again. Pour the biscuit crumbs into a bowl.

2. Melt the butter in a saucepan over medium heat, then pour the melted butter over biscuit crumbs and mix thoroughly. Tip the biscuit mixture into a spring-form cake tin and spread it out, then press it down firmly with the back of a spoon. Make sure you press some up the sides as well. The biscuit crust should be about 5 mm (¼ in) thick all over. Refrigerate for 20 minutes while you prepare the filling.

3. To make the filling, put the cream cheese in a bowl and mash it up with a fork. Add the lemon juice and condensed milk and beat with an egg beater until the mixture is smooth. Pour the cheese mixture into the pie dish and smooth over gently with a spoon. Put the cheesecake in the refrigerator and leave to set for at least 4 hours.

4. When ready to serve, decorate with whipped cream and thinly sliced lemon rind.

serves 10

Strawberry shortcake

125 g (4½ oz) butter, plus extra for greasing
125 g (4½ oz) caster (superfine) sugar
1 egg
1 teaspoon vanilla extract
175 g (6 oz) plain (all-purpose) flour
30 g (1 oz) cornflour (corn starch)
2 teaspoons baking powder
2 tablespoons milk
450 g (1 lb) strawberries, crushed leaving some whole, to decorate
250 ml (8 fl oz / 1 cup) fresh cream, whipped

1. Preheat the oven to 180°C/350°F/Gas mark 4. Grease a 20 cm (8 in) springform cake tin (pan).
2. In a bowl, cream the butter and sugar together until light and fluffy. Add the egg and vanilla and beat well.
3. Into another bowl, sift the dry ingredients. Add a spoonful at a time to the butter and sugar mixture, alternating with the milk and beating well after each addition.
4. Pour the batter into the prepared tin and bake for 30–35 minutes, until a skewer inserted into the middle of the cake comes out clean. Set aside on a wire rack for 10 minutes.
5. Turn out the cake from the tin and allow to stand until quite cold. Cut the cake in half horizontally, through the centre. Cover the lower half with whipped cream and crushed strawberries in separate layers. Place the other half on top and cover it with whipped cream and berries, either whole or halved, placing the cut side down on the cream.

serves 6–8

Apple cake

150 g (5 oz) butter
200 g (7 oz) sugar
3 eggs, separated
7 oz (200 g/1¾ cups) plain (all-purpose) flour
2 teaspoons baking powder
2 tablespoons ground almonds (almond meal)
pinch of salt
¼ teaspoon nutmeg
¼ teaspoon ground cinnamon
6 cooking apples, peeled, cored and sliced and brushed with 2 tablespoons lemon juice

1. Preheat the oven to 180°C/350°F/Gas mark 4. Grease and line a 23 cm (9 in) round cake tin (pan).
2. Beat the butter and 150 g (5 oz) of the sugar together, in a mixing bowl, until thick and pale. Add the egg yolks one at a time, beating well after each addition.
3. In another clean, grease-free bowl, whisk the egg whites until firm peaks form.
4. In another bowl, mix the flour, baking powder, ground almonds, salt and spices.
5. Add half the egg whites and flour mixture to the batter and whisk together carefully. Repeat with the remaining ingredients and mix well.
6. Pour the batter into the prepared tin. Press the apple slices into the batter in a circular pattern, and dust with the remaining sugar. Bake for 50 minutes, until golden. Leave to set in the tin for 10 minutes, then turn out onto a wire rack to go cold.

makes 1 cake

Yule log

5 eggs, separated
60 g (2 oz / ¼ cup) caster (superfine) sugar, plus
extra for dusting
100 g (3½ oz) dark (bittersweet) chocolate, melted
and cooled
2 tablespoons self-raising (self-rising) flour, sifted
2 tablespoons unsweetened cocoa powder, sifted

FOR THE WHITE CHOCOLATE FILLING
60 g (2 oz) white chocolate
160 ml (5½ fl oz / ⅔ cup) thickened cream

FOR THE CHOCOLATE FROSTING
200 g (7 oz) dark (bittersweet) chocolate, melted
60 g (2 oz) butter, melted, plus extra for greasing

1. Preheat the oven to 180°C/350°F/Gas mark 4. Grease and line a 26 x 32 cm (10 x 13 in) Swiss roll tin (jelly roll pan).
2. Put the egg yolks and sugar in a bowl and beat until thick and pale. Stir in the melted chocolate, flour and cocoa powder.
3. Put the egg whites in a clean, grease-free bowl and beat until stiff peaks form. Fold the egg whites carefully into the chocolate mixture.
4. Pour into the prepared tin and bake for 15 minutes, or until firm. Turn immediately onto a clean and damp dish towel dusted with superfine sugar and roll up tightly. Set aside to cool.
5. To make the filling, put the white chocolate in a heatproof bowl set over a pan of simmering water and heat, stirring, until smooth. Add the cream and stir until combined. Cover and chill until thickened and spreadable.
6. Unroll the cake and spread with filling, leaving a 1 cm (½ in) border. Re-roll the cake.
7. To make the frosting, combine the melted chocolate and butter and mix until combined. Spread over the roll, then use a fork to roughly texture the icing. Keep refrigerated. Serve cold.

serves 8

Sacher torte

250 g (9 oz) butter, softened
340 g (12 oz / 1½ cups) brown sugar
2 teaspoons vanilla extract
2 eggs, lightly beaten
175 g (6 oz / 1½ cups) plain (all-purpose) flour
150 g (5¼ oz / ⅔ cup) unsweetened cocoa powder
¾ teaspoon baking powder
280 ml (10 fl oz / 1½ cups) buttermilk
85 g (3 oz / ½ cup) apricot jam

FOR THE CHOCOLATE FROSTING
200 g (7 oz) dark (bittersweet) chocolate, broken into pieces
200 g (7 oz) butter, chopped

1. Preheat the oven to 180°C/350°F/Gas mark 4. Lightly grease two 23 cm (9 in) round cake tins (pans).
2. Put the butter, sugar and vanilla in a bowl and beat until light and fluffy. Gradually beat in the eggs.
3. Sift the flour, cocoa powder and baking powder into the butter mixture. Add the buttermilk and mix well to combine.
4. Pour the batter into the prepared tins and bake for 25 minutes, or until cooked when tested with a skewer. Allow to set for 5 minutes before turning out onto a wire rack to cool.
5. To make the frosting, put chocolate and butter in a heatproof bowl set over a saucepan of simmering water and heat, stirring, until the mixture is smooth. Remove the bowl from the pan and set aside to cool until the mixture thickens to a spreadable consistency.
6. To assemble the cake, place one cake on a serving plate and spread with jam. Top with the remaining cake and spread the top and sides with most of the frosting. Place remaining frosting in a piping bag and pipe swirls around edge of cake.

serves 8–10

Chocolate pound cake

175g (6 oz) butter, softened, plus extra for greasing
245 g (8¾ oz / 1¼ cups) caster (superfine) sugar
3 teaspoons vanilla extract
3 eggs, lightly beaten
175 g (6 oz / 1½ cups) self-raising (self-rising) flour
60 g (2 oz / ½ cup) plain (all-purpose) flour
60 g(2 oz / ½ cup) unsweeetened cocoa powder
280 ml (10 fl oz / 1¼ cups) milk
icing (confectioners') sugar, for dusting

1. Preheat the oven to 190°C/380°F/Gas mark 5. Grease and line a 20 cm (7¾ in) square cake tin (pan).
2. Put the butter, sugar and vanilla in a bowl and beat until light and fluffy. Gradually beat in the eggs.
3. Sift the flours and cocoa powder together into another bowl. Fold the flour mixture and milk alternately into the butter mixture.
4. Pour the batter into the prepared cake tin and bake for 55 minutes, or until a skewer, when inserted into the centre, comes out clean. Let stand for 10 minutes before turning out onto a wire rack to cool. Serve with chocolate sauce and cream. Dust with icing sugar.

serves 8

Sponge cake

225 g (8 oz) butter, softened, plus extra for greasing
2 teaspoons vanilla extract
1 teaspoon finely grated lemon zest
400 g (14 oz / 2 cups) caster (superfine) sugar
6 eggs
175 g (6 oz / 1½ cups) plain (all-purpose) flour
115 g (4 oz / 1 cup) self-raising (self-rising) flour
250 ml (8 fl oz / 1 cup) natural (plain) yogurt

FOR LEMON FROSTING
175 g (6 oz / 1½ cups) icing (confectioners')
sugar, sifted
1 tablespoon lemon juice
2 tablespoons butter, softened
2 tablespoons dessicated (dry, unsweetened, shredded)
coconut, toasted

1. Preheat the oven to 160°C/325°F/Gas mark 3. Grease and line a 23 cm (9 in) square cake tin (pan).
2. Put the butter, vanilla extract and lemon zest in a bowl and beat until light and fluffy. Gradually add the sugar, beating well after each addition until the mixture is creamy. Add the eggs one at a time, beating well after each addition.
3. Sift the flours together into another bowl. Fold the flours and yogurt, alternately, into the butter mixture. Spoon the batter into the prepared tin and bake for 1 hour, or until the cake is cooked when tested with a skewer. Leave to set for 10 minutes before turning out onto a wire rack to cool completely.
4. To make the frosting, put the confectioners' sugar, lemon juice and butter in a bowl and mix until smooth. Add a little more lemon juice, if necessary. Spread the frosting over the cake and sprinkle with coconut.

makes 1 cake

Fruity carrot loaf

*115 g (4 oz / 1 cup) wholemeal (whole wheat)
self-raising (self-rising) flour
60 g (2 oz / ½ cup) rye flour
100 g (3½ oz / ½ cup) demerara (raw) sugar
½ teaspoon salt
½ tablespoon baking soda (bicarbonate of soda)
1 teaspoon ground cinnamon
½ cup crushed pineapple, undrained
175 g (6 oz / 1 cup) grated carrot
2 eggs*

*125 ml (4 fl oz / ½ cup) oil, plus extra for greasing
1 teaspoon vanilla extract
60 g (2 oz / ½ cup) chopped walnuts*

LEMON GLACÉ TOPPING
*115 g (4 oz / 1 cup) icing (confectioners') sugar
1 teaspoon butter
vanilla extract
1 tablespoon lemon juice
½ teaspoon lemon zest*

1. Preheat the oven to 180°C/350°F/Gas mark 4. Grease an 20 x 15 cm (8 x 6 in) loaf tin (pan) and line with baking paper.
2. Sift the flours, sugar, salt, baking soda and cinnamon into a mixing bowl. Add the crushed pineapple, carrot, eggs, oil and vanilla and beat until well combined. Stir the chopped walnuts into the carrot mixture. Spoon the batter into prepared tin. Bake for 25–30 minutes, or until a skewer inserted in the centre comes out clean.
3. Remove from the oven and allow to cool in the tin for 5 minutes before turning out onto a wire rack to cool completely.
4. To make the lemon glacé topping, put the sifted icing sugar in a heatproof bowl set over a pan of simmering water. Make a well in the centre, and add the butter, a few drops of vanilla extract and the lemon juice. Stir slowly until all sugar has been incorporated and the topping is smooth and shiny. Coat the cake top while still warm.

makes 1 loaf

Christmas cake

250 g (9 oz) dates
250 g (9 oz) raisins
225 g (8 oz) currants
225 g (8 oz) dried pineapple
225 g (8 oz) dried figs
750 ml (24 fl oz / 3 cups) water
175 g (6 oz) wholemeal (whole wheat) flour
340 g (12 oz) self-raising (self-rising) flour, sifted
175 ml (6 fl oz / ¾ cup) olive oil, plus extra for greasing

1. Chop all the fruit, tip into a bowl, pour over the water and leave to soak for 1 hour. Drain the water, reserving 125 ml (4 fl oz / ½ cup) of the liquid.
2. Preheat the oven to 130°C (265°F / Gas ¾). In a bowl, mix the flour, reserved water and oil to a soft dough. Add the soaked fruit and mix thoroughly. Spread the mixture into a greased 25 cm (10 in) square cake tin (pan) and cover with foil. Bake for 3½ hours, removing the foil after 3 hours of cooking. The cake is ready when a wooden skewer inserted into the middle of the cake comes out clean.

serves 16–20

Simple brownies

5 oz (150 g) butter, softened, plus extra for greasing
115 g (4 oz / ½ cup) honey, warmed
2 eggs, lightly beaten
200 g (7 oz / 1¾ cups) self-raising (self-rising) flour, sifted
160 g (5½ oz / ⅔ cup) brown sugar
125g (4½ oz) semisweet (dark) chocolate, melted and cooled
icing (confectioners') sugar, sifted

1. Preheat the oven to 180°C/350°F/Gas mark 4. Grease and line a 23 cm (9 in) square cake tin (pan).
2. Put the butter, honey, eggs, flour, sugar, chocolate and 1 tablespoon of water in a food processor and process until the ingredients are combined.
3. Spoon the batter into the prepared tin and bake for 30–35 minutes, or until cooked through. Leave to stand in the tin for 5 minutes before turning out onto a wire rack to cool completely.
4. Dust with confectioners' sugar and cut into squares.

makes 25

Caramel squares

100 g (3½ oz) butter, plus extra for greasing
45 g (1½ oz) sugar
85 g (3 oz/¾ cup) cornflour (corn starch), sifted
85 g (3 oz/¾ cup) plain (all-purpose) flour, sifted, plus extra for dusting

FOR THE FILLING AND TOPPING
115 g (4 oz/½ cup) butter
115 g (4 oz/½ cup) brown sugar
2 tablespoons honey
400 g (14 oz) can sweetened condensed milk
1 teaspoon vanilla extract
200 g (7 oz) dark (bittersweet) chocolate, melted

1. Preheat the oven to 180°C/350°F/Gas mark 4. Grease and line a 20 x 30 cm (8 x 12 in) shallow cake tin (pan).
2. To make the base, beat the butter and sugar in a mixing bowl until light and fluffy. Mix in the cornflour and flour. Turn out onto a lightly floured surface and knead briefly, then press into the prepared tin and bake for 25 minutes, or until firm.
3. To make the filling, put the butter, brown sugar and honey in a saucepan and melt over medium heat, stirring constantly until the sugar dissolves and the ingredients are combined. Bring to the boil and simmer for 7 minutes. Beat in the condensed milk and vanilla extract. Pour the filling over the base and bake for 20 minutes. Set aside to cool completely.
4. Spread melted chocolate over the filling. Set aside until firm, then cut into squares.

makes 24

Shortbread cookies

125 g (4½ oz) butter
60 g (2 oz) caster (superfine) sugar
1 teaspoon vanilla extract
100 g (3½ oz) plain (all-purpose) flour
60 g (2 oz) rice flour
25 g (¾ oz) cornflour (cornstarch)

1. In a bowl, cream the butter and sugar, then add the vanilla. While mixing, slowly add the flours and form a dough.
2. Place the mixture onto a baking tray covered with baking paper. Freeze the tray and dough for 10 minutes (or refrigerate for 20 minutes). Preheat the oven to 200°C/400°F/Gas mark 6.
3. Remove the mixture from the freezer and cut into cookie shape. Bake for about 10 minutes, or until golden.

makes 16

Cinnamon cookies

225 g (8 oz) butter, softened, plus extra for greasing
115 g (4 oz) caster (superfine) sugar
1 teaspoon vanilla extract
340 g (12 oz/3 cups) plain (all-purpose) flour
2 teaspoons ground cinnamon
salt
175 g (6 oz/1½ cups) icing (confectioners') sugar

1. In a bowl, beat together the butter, sugar and vanilla extract. Stir in the flour, 1 teaspoon of cinnamon and a pinch of salt to make a soft dough. Cover and refrigerate for 1 hour.
2. Preheat the oven to 350°F/180°C/Gas mark 4. Grease two baking sheets.
3. Form the mixture into 2.5 cm (1 in) balls and place on a prepared baking sheet, leaving space between each one. Bake for 15 minutes. Leave to set on the baking sheets for a few minutes, then transfer to a wire rack to cool.
4. Mix together the icing sugar and remaining cinnamon and dust over the cookies before serving.

makes 24

Almond biscotti

oil, for greasing
2 large eggs
100 g (3½ oz / ½ cup) caster (superfine) sugar
1 teaspoon vanilla extract
1 teaspoon grated orange zest
180 g (6½ oz / 1²/₃ cups) plain (all-purpose) flour, plus extra for dusting
½ teaspoon baking powder
85 g (3 oz / ¾ cup) blanched almonds, lightly toasted
egg white, for glazing

1. Preheat the oven to 350°F/180°C/Gas mark 4. Grease two baking sheets and dust with flour.
2. In a mixing bowl, beat the eggs, sugar, vanilla extract and orange zest until thick and creamy.
3. Sift the flour and baking powder into the egg mixture and fold in with the almonds.
4. Knead on a floured surface until smooth. Divide the dough in half. Shape each piece into a log about 2 in (5 cm) wide and 2.5 cm (1 in) thick. Place on a baking sheet. Brush with egg white.
5. Bake for 30 minutes, or until firm. Cool for 10 minutes. Cut each log diagonally into 1 cm (³/₈ in) thick slices. Place on the baking trays. Bake for 20–30 minutes, or until dry and crisp. Cool on wire racks.

makes 30

Cook's notes

Cooking is not an exact science; one does not require finely calibrated scales, pipettes and scientific equipment to cook. Baking, on the other hand, does require exactitude when measuring ingredients, baking tin (pan) sizes and cooking temperatures.

The measurements given in the book are made up of metric, imperial and cups. The measures are not interchangeable so if you begin the recipe weighing ingredients in metric, you must stick to that measure throughout.

Eggs are medium in size unless stated otherwise.

Fluid measures

60 ml = ¼ cup
85 ml = ⅓ cup
125 ml = ½ cup
250 ml = 1 cup
500 ml = 2 cups
1 litre = 1¾ pints

Solid measures

10 g = ⅓ oz
20 g = ⅔ oz
30 g = 1 oz
45 g = 1½ oz
60 g = 2 oz
75 g = 2½ oz
100 g = 3½ oz
115 g = 4 oz
150 g = 5 oz
160 g = 5½ oz
175 g = 6 oz
200 g = 7 oz
225 g = 8 oz
300 g = 10½ oz
350 g = 12½ oz
400 g = 14 oz
500 g = 1 lb 2 oz
750 g = 1½ lb
1 kg = 2 lb

Index

First published in 2015 by New Holland Publishers Pty Ltd
London • Sydney • Auckland

The Chandlery Unit 009 50 Westminster Bridge Road London SE1 7QY United Kingdom
1/66 Gibbes Street Chatswood NSW 2067 Australia
5 39 Woodside Ave Northcote Auckland New Zealand

www.newhollandpublishers.com

A record of this book is held at the British Library and the National Library of Australia.

ISBN 9781742576664

Managing Director: Fiona Schultz
Editor: Simona Hill
Designer: Lorena Susak
Production Director: Olga Dementiev
Printer: Toppan Leefung Printing Ltd

10 9 8 7 6 5 4 3 2 1

Keep up with New Holland Publishers on Facebook
www.facebook.com/NewHollandPublishers